BUILD YOUR OWN
PAPER
AIR FORCE

D0490672

3 1 OCT 2014

1 9 FEB 2015

1 2 MAY 2015

2 0 JUN 2017

0 8 FEB 2018

- 7 MAR 2018

- 6 APR 2018

- 8 SEP 2018

WITHDRAWN FROM STOCK

BUILD YOUR OWN
PAPER
AIR FORCE

AMAZING PLANE DESIGNS TO PRINT, FOLD AND FLY

TREVOR BOUNFORD

ILEX

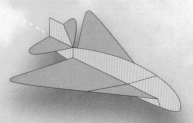

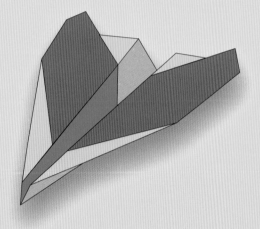

BUILD YOUR OWN PAPER AIR FORCE
First published in the United Kingdom in 2010 by
I L E X
210 High Street
Lewes
East Sussex BN7 2NS
www.ilex-press.com

Copyright © 2010 The Ilex Press Limited

Publisher: Alastair Campbell
Creative Director: Peter Bridgewater
Managing Editor: Nick Jones
Senior Project Editor: Chris Gatcum
Editors: Tim Seelig and Ellie Wilson
Art Director: Julie Weir
Designers: Jonathan Raimes and Ginny Zeal

Any copy of this book issued by the publisher is sold subject to
the condition that it shall not by way of trade or otherwise be lent,
resold, hired out, or otherwise circulated without the publisher's prior
consent in any form of binding or cover other than that in which it
is published and without a similar condition including these words
being imposed on a subsequent purchaser.

British Library Cataloguing-in-Publication Data
A catalogue record for this book is available from
the British Library

ISBN: 978-1-907579-02-8

All rights reserved. No part of this publication may be reproduced
or used in any form, or by any means – graphic, electronic, or
mechanical, including photocopying, recording, or information
storage-and-retrieval systems – without the prior permission of
the publisher.

10 9 8 7 6 5 4 3

Printed in China

Colour Origination by Ivy Press Reprographics.

Leabharlann
Contae na...

contents

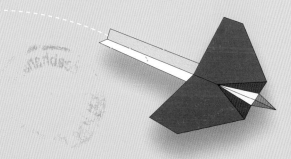

6

introduction

Almost everyone knows how to make at least one paper plane—usually the one their dad taught them—but there are countless different models and variations.

In 1967, *Scientific American* ran an international contest to find the best paper airplane of the time and was swamped with entries. In all, there were almost 12,000 models entered by over 5,000 contestants from 28 countries.

This book and CD includes templates for 35 different models, along with a whole range of color schemes, background textures, and images that will let you create hundreds of variations of these planes using any picture editing software—an entire air force in fact!

aircraft construction

On the base template for each model are lines indicating the method of fold required for constructing the plane. You need to make the first fold in the right direction (see below) otherwise the fold markings will be concealed within the model.

A valley fold is made as if you were closing a book—so the folded sheet becomes a valley.

A hill or mountain fold is made the opposite way, so the fold becomes a mountain ridge.

A crease requires the paper segment to be folded, flattened, and then unfolded to leave a clean line.

Arrows on the instructional diagrams show in which direction the segment is moved.

The "push" or "tuck" arrow usually means that you have to manipulate a previously creased segment inside or behind another segment.

Another type of arrow shows when to turn the paper over so you can work from the other side.

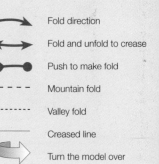

→	Fold direction
↔	Fold and unfold to crease
⊶●	Push to make fold
- - - -	Mountain fold
....	Valley fold
	Creased line
⇨	Turn the model over

Mountain fold

Valley fold

---

tips

1. Be very careful when cutting out the templates. Some of the more complex planes need curved lines cutting. You will need a sharp craft knife and a proper cutting mat. Exercise caution at all times for your own safety, and keep sharp implements out of reach of children.

2. Work on a good, clean surface with plenty of light—a desk light, or other working light that can be directed, is ideal.

3. Make sure folds and creases are made precisely. Use the edge of a good quality ruler—ideally a metal ruler—to help fold along a line. Lay the edge of the ruler against the line of the fold and pull the exposed segment up firmly against the ruler's edge. Don't pull too hard or the paper may begin to tear. In some cases it may help to make the opposite type of fold and then reverse it. For example, if you

need a mountain fold but cannot see the fold indicator, make a valley fold, flatten to crease, then turn the model over and make a valley fold from the other side—which is actually the mountain fold you wanted.

4. You don't have to keep the paper oriented exactly as the instruction diagram. In fact, it will almost certainly be easier to rotate the paper and model to suit your folding technique. Just be sure to position it so that you can see where the edges and folds need to be for precise construction.

5. Once the paper is folded, make a clean sharp crease by running the flat of your thumbnail along the fold.

6. Allow for the thickness of the paper as you build multiple folds. In particular, nose sections of some planes will build up a substantial thickness. Where the instruction

is to bring the edge of the paper to the center crease, let it fall a paper thickness or two short of the crease so that the edge won't push over and obstruct the opposite piece as the folds build up.

7. With all planes, it is best to print out and make a trial version, or more than one version, in order to get familiar with the technique for the model before you try to make one with your best paper.

8. Almost all the models can be made with standard office paper. One or two—such as The Eagle and The Dart—work well on very light paper (I've recycled old telephone directory pages to make them). Almost all the cut out planes need heavier paper—only The Scales and The Twins work with lighter paper.

8

coloring the planes

On the CD, there are colored versions of the templates to show where color can be added. As the planes are folded together, some parts are not visible and therefore do not need coloring (which saves your ink). Also on the CD are sample color arrangements, and designs that can be added to the models before printing.

Using a basic paint package such as Adobe Photoshop Elements, you can change the color using either the colored templates or the versions with fold lines. However, if you color over the fold lines you won't be able to see what type of fold is needed, so you may want to have a "blank" template to use as a guide to folding the colored one.

1. Open the model you want to color in your paint program—working with MS Windows, double-click the model template file, then select the software program you want to use to open the file.

2. Choose the color you intend to use, then select the **Paint Bucket** tool and click in the area you want colored—the fold lines have a continuous line underlaying them in order to set a bounding box for the color area.

3. Continue adding color to other segments as desired. Once you have filled an area with color, you can change it again using the **Paint Bucket** tool, making sure a replacement color is selected first Remember that printing large areas of full-strength color will use up the ink supplies in your printer a lot faster.

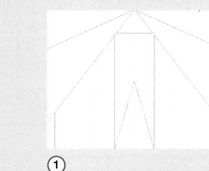

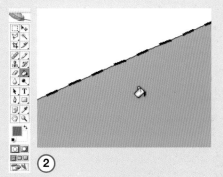

adding emblems

1. Adding one of the many pictorial emblems is simple. Open the file with the emblem you want, select all of it (or just the part of the emblem you need), and copy it to the pasteboard. Open the model template and paste the emblem in. You can then drag the emblem wherever you want it.

2. Once in position you can delete any unwanted parts of the emblem file, or recolor those parts to the base color of the segment on which you pasted the emblem. Clone the emblem, or paste again, if you want a duplicate emblem to position symmetrically.

3. You can also resize emblems. This is particularly useful if you want to add them elsewhere on the model, for example if you want an identity mark on both wings, and a smaller one on the tail.

4. You should also rotate the emblems so they will read correctly on the completed model.

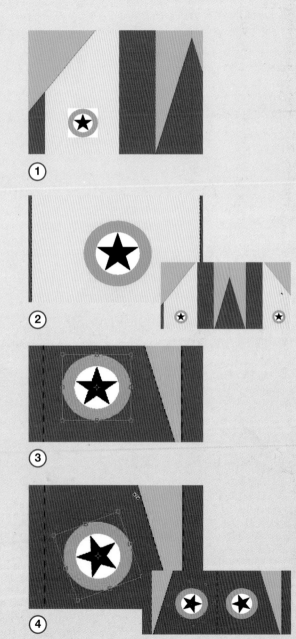

flight theory

Paper gliders follow the physical laws that govern the flight of any craft—lift keeps the craft up while gravity pulls it down, and thrust drives it forward while drag pulls it back.

A successful plane maximizes lift while minimizing gravitational pull, and minimizes drag to maximize thrust. Depending on the plane's design, this allows it stay aloft as long as possible or to execute some stunt maneuver before reaching the ground.

Be sure to make the plane as carefully as possible, flattening all creases and aligning folded segments precisely. Adjust the trim of the model to get the best performance. You do this by bending the wings up or down, or ensuring they are flat, according to the trim guidelines.

Once you have successfully flown a model, you may want to experiment with the trim to make the plane fly slightly differently. For example, folding up a wing tip slightly might make the plane turn to one side.

Also experiment with launch technique. Some craft fly better when launched gently, while others need a firm throw. Try throwing the plane vertically to see if it levels out.

It is important to choose your flying area carefully. Don't launch in a room where items may be knocked down and damaged. Take care when other people are present and never throw a plane at another person. Even paper can cause injury—especially when folded.

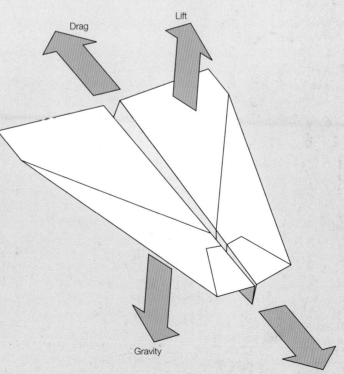

Drag

Lift

Gravity

Thrust

part 1
single sheet folded planes

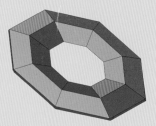

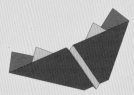

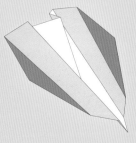

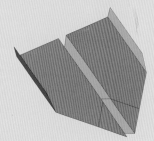

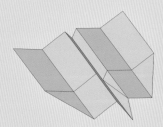

missilis

Flight Path:	Flight Speed:	Throwing Technique:	Flight Correction:	trim view from rear
Straight	Medium	Pinch the undersection at the front of the plane and throw normally	Plane will usually fly easily—if not check the trim	Wings almost level, raised slightly upwards

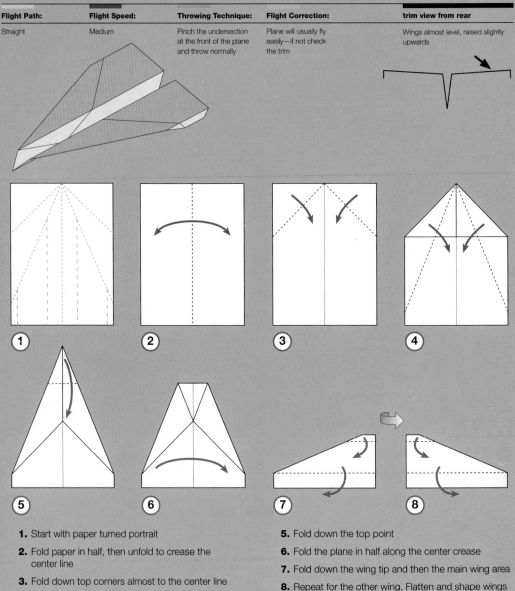

1. Start with paper turned portrait

2. Fold paper in half, then unfold to crease the center line

3. Fold down top corners almost to the center line

4. Fold down top edges to the center line

5. Fold down the top point

6. Fold the plane in half along the center crease

7. Fold down the wing tip and then the main wing area

8. Repeat for the other wing. Flatten and shape wings to form the finished model

14

SINGLE SHEET FOLDED PLANES

the spear
curis

Flight Path:	Flight Speed:	Throwing Technique:	Flight Correction:	trim view from rear
Straight	Medium	Pinch the undersection at the front of the plane and throw normally	If plane stalls, throw more gently. If plane rocks, adjust the inner wing angle up or down slightly and try again	Wing edges raised quite steeply

Inner wing almost level, lowered slightly downwards

1. Start with paper turned portrait

2. Fold paper in half, then unfold to crease the center line

3. Fold down top corners almost to the center line

4. Fold down top edges to the center line

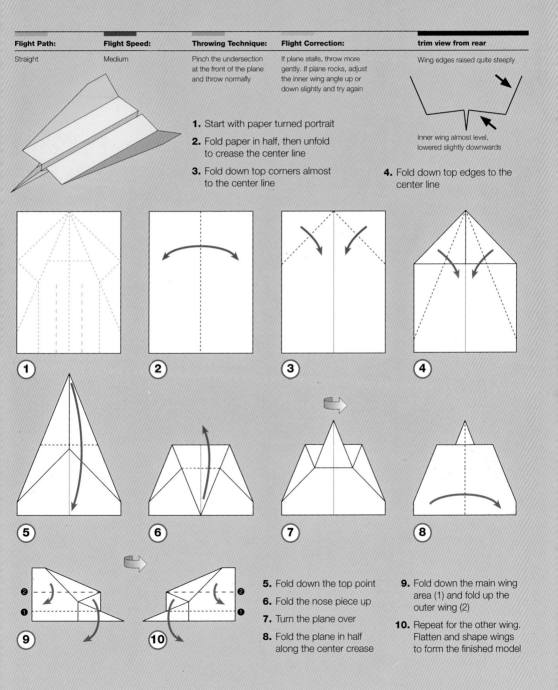

5. Fold down the top point

6. Fold the nose piece up

7. Turn the plane over

8. Fold the plane in half along the center crease

9. Fold down the main wing area (1) and fold up the outer wing (2)

10. Repeat for the other wing. Flatten and shape wings to form the finished model

the fly

musca

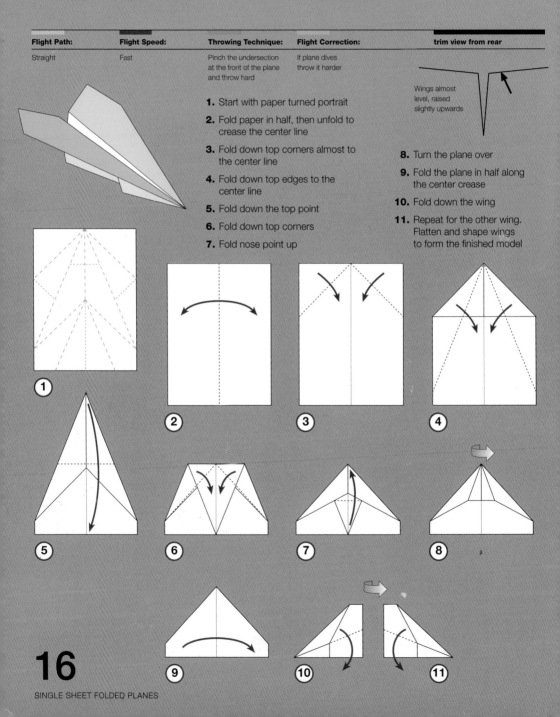

Flight Path:	Flight Speed:	Throwing Technique:	Flight Correction:	trim view from rear
Straight	Fast	Pinch the undersection at the front of the plane and throw hard	If plane dives throw it harder	

Wings almost level, raised slightly upwards

1. Start with paper turned portrait

2. Fold paper in half, then unfold to crease the center line

3. Fold down top corners almost to the center line

4. Fold down top edges to the center line

5. Fold down the top point

6. Fold down top corners

7. Fold nose point up

8. Turn the plane over

9. Fold the plane in half along the center crease

10. Fold down the wing

11. Repeat for the other wing. Flatten and shape wings to form the finished model

16

SINGLE SHEET FOLDED PLANES

the dart
telum

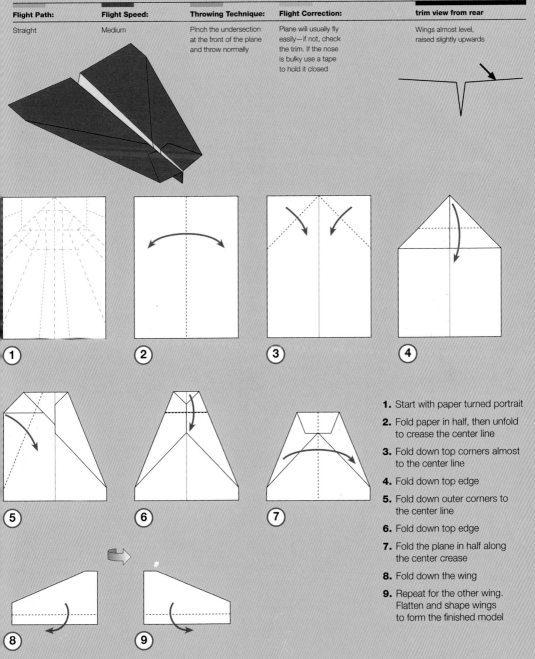

Flight Path:	Flight Speed:	Throwing Technique:	Flight Correction:	trim view from rear
Straight	Medium	Pinch the undersection at the front of the plane and throw normally	Plane will usually fly easily—if not, check the trim. If the nose is bulky use a tape to hold it closed	Wings almost level, raised slightly upwards

1. Start with paper turned portrait

2. Fold paper in half, then unfold to crease the center line

3. Fold down top corners almost to the center line

4. Fold down top edge

5. Fold down outer corners to the center line

6. Fold down top edge

7. Fold the plane in half along the center crease

8. Fold down the wing

9. Repeat for the other wing. Flatten and shape wings to form the finished model

the dragon

draco

Flight Path:	Flight Speed:	Throwing Technique:	Flight Correction:	trim view from rear
Straight	Medium	Pinch the undersection at the front of the plane and throw normally	If plane dives, throw more gently	Wings need to be raised upwards

1. Start with paper turned portrait
2. Fold paper in half, then unfold to crease the center line
3. Fold down top corners almost to the center line
4. Fold down the top point
5. Fold down top corners to the center line (20mm up from the point)

6. Fold up point to overlap
7. Turn the plane over
8. Fold the plane in half along the center crease

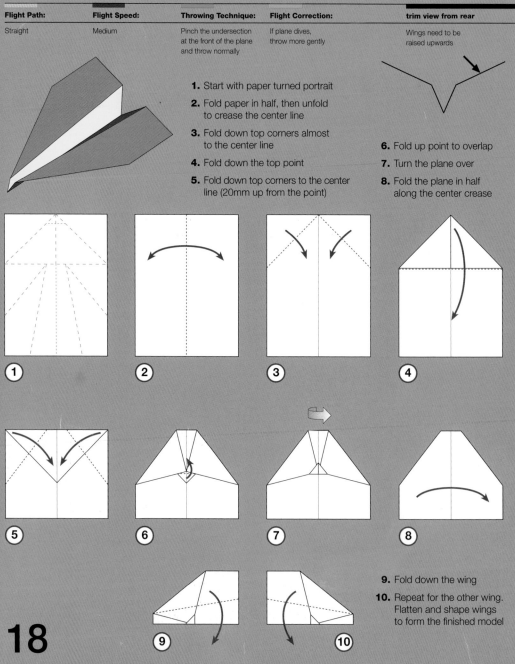

9. Fold down the wing
10. Repeat for the other wing. Flatten and shape wings to form the finished model

18

SINGLE SHEET FOLDED PLANES

the bull
taurus

Flight Path:	Flight Speed:	Throwing Technique:	Flight Correction:		trim view from rear
Straight	Slow	Pinch the undersection at the front of the plane and throw normally	Plane will usually fly easily—if not, check the trim		Wings almost level, raised slightly upwards

1. Start with paper turned portrait
2. Fold paper in half, then unfold to crease the center line
3. Fold down top corners almost to the center line
4. Turn the plane over
5. Fold down the top corners and allow the triangles to come out from underneath
6. Fold down top point
7. Turn the plane over
8. Fold the plane in half along the center crease

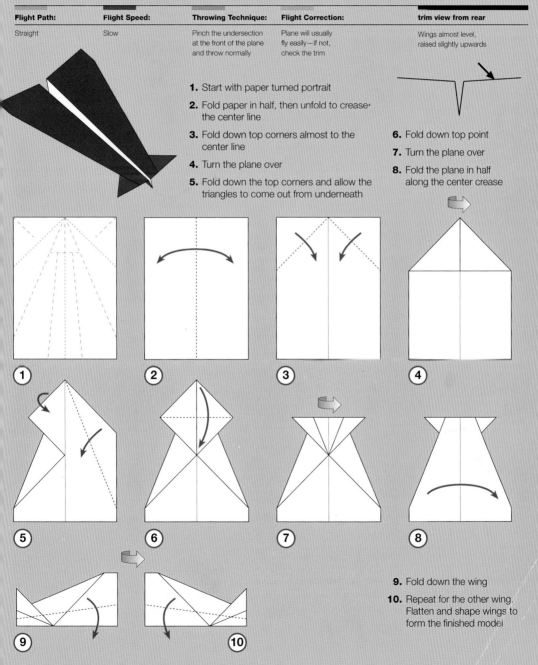

9. Fold down the wing
10. Repeat for the other wing. Flatten and shape wings to form the finished model

pisces

Flight Path:	Flight Speed:	Throwing Technique:	Flight Correction:	trim view from top
Spins downwards	Medium	Make sure the plane is held so it is sideways (not with the nose pointing down). Hold the edge on one side and then let go	The plane should fly easily	When flying hold from one edge

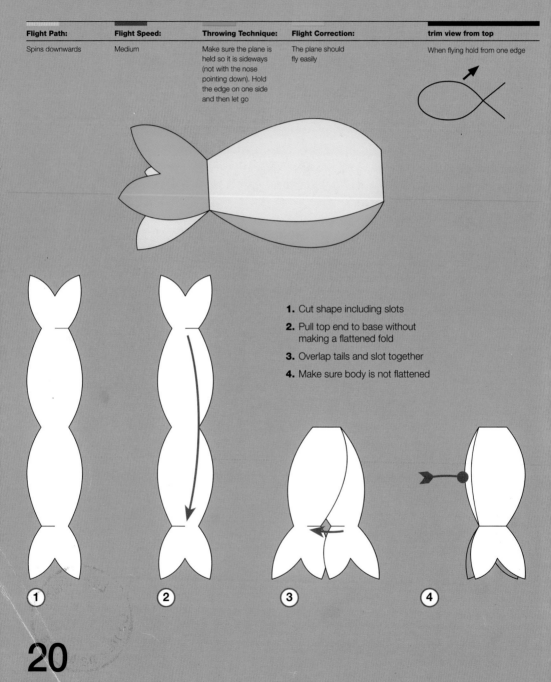

1. Cut shape including slots
2. Pull top end to base without making a flattened fold
3. Overlap tails and slot together
4. Make sure body is not flattened

Flight Path:	Flight Speed:	Throwing Technique:	Flight Correction:	trim view from rear
Spins downwards	Medium	Hold the plane at the bottom section and let go	Plane will usually fly easily—if not, check the trim	Wings need to be raised upwards

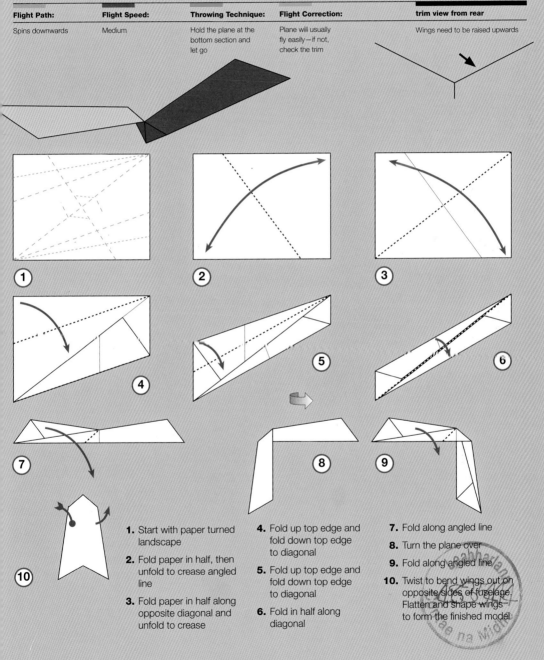

1. Start with paper turned landscape

2. Fold paper in half, then unfold to crease angled line

3. Fold paper in half along opposite diagonal and unfold to crease

4. Fold up top edge and fold down top edge to diagonal

5. Fold up top edge and fold down top edge to diagonal

6. Fold in half along diagonal

7. Fold along angled line

8. Turn the plane over

9. Fold along angled line

10. Twist to bend wings out on opposite sides of fuselage. Flatten and shape wings to form the finished model

corvus

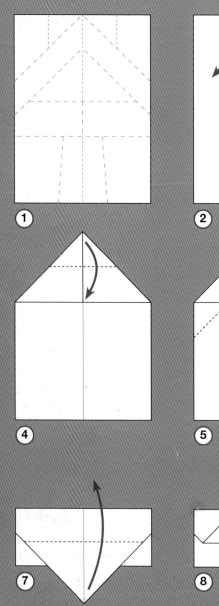
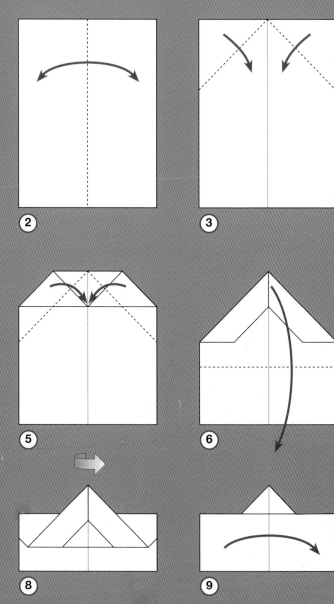

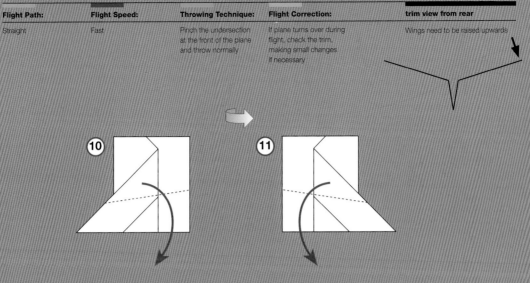

Flight Path:	Flight Speed:	Throwing Technique:	Flight Correction:	trim view from rear
Straight	Fast	Pinch the undersection at the front of the plane and throw normally	If plane turns over during flight, check the trim, making small changes if necessary	Wings need to be raised upwards

1. Start with paper turned portrait
2. Fold paper in half, then unfold to crease the center line
3. Fold down top corners almost to the center line
4. Fold down the top point
5. Fold down top corners to the center line
6. Fold down top point to overlap base of paper

7. Fold up nose piece
8. Turn the plane over
9. Fold the plane in half along the center crease
10. Fold down the wing
11. Repeat for the other wing. Flatten and shape wings to form the finished model

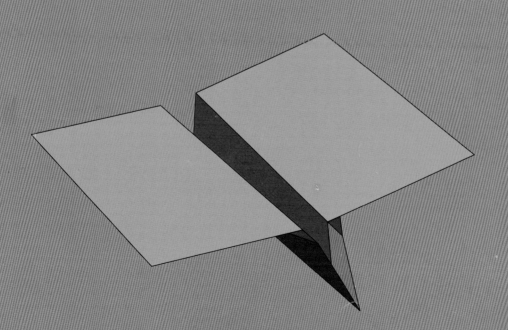

accipiter

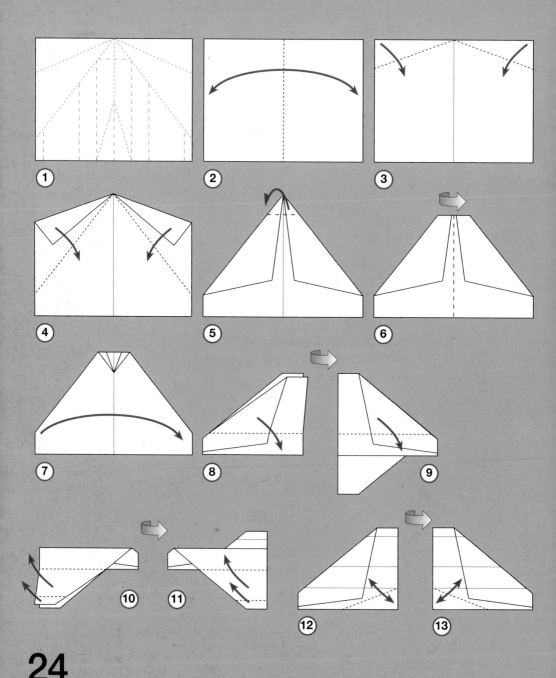

Straight	Slow	Pinch the undersection at the middle of the plane and throw normally	If plane dives, throw more gently. If plane is not flying well, check the trim looks like the diagram, in particular with the outer wings being straight	

Tail fold should look like this

Outer wings should be as level as possible

Stabilizers need to be vertical

(14)

1. Start with paper turned landscape

2. Fold paper in half, then unfold to crease the center line

3. Fold down top corners

4. Fold down top edges

5. Fold the top point behind the plane

6. Turn plane over

7. Fold the plane in half along the center crease

8. Fold down the wing and turn the model over

9. Fold down the other wing

10. Fold up the wing tip and then the main wing area

11. Repeat for the other wing

12. Flatten wings, crease tail section with valley fold, then turn the model over

13. Crease tail section on opposite side

14. Push the tail section up between the wings. Flatten tail section and reshape wings to form the finished model

cygnus

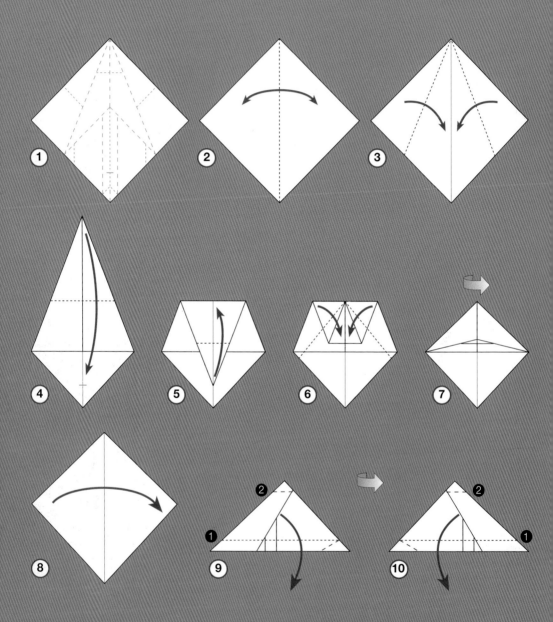

1. Start with a square of paper turned through 45

2. Fold paper in half, then unfold to crease the center line

3. Fold down top corners almost to the center line

4. Fold down the top point to the mark

5. Fold nose point up

6. Fold down top corners to the center line

7. Turn the plane over

8. Fold the plane in half along the center crease

9. Fold down the wing (1) and then fold up the wing tip (2)

10. Repeat for the other wing then open out wings

11. Crease tail section with valley fold then turn the model over

12. Repeat tail crease then push up to form tail. Reshape wings and trim to form the finished model

Tail fold should look like this

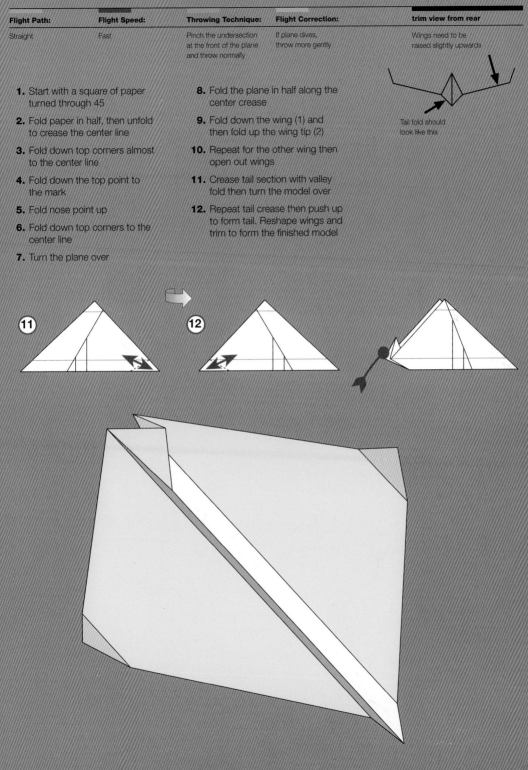

the eagle
aquila

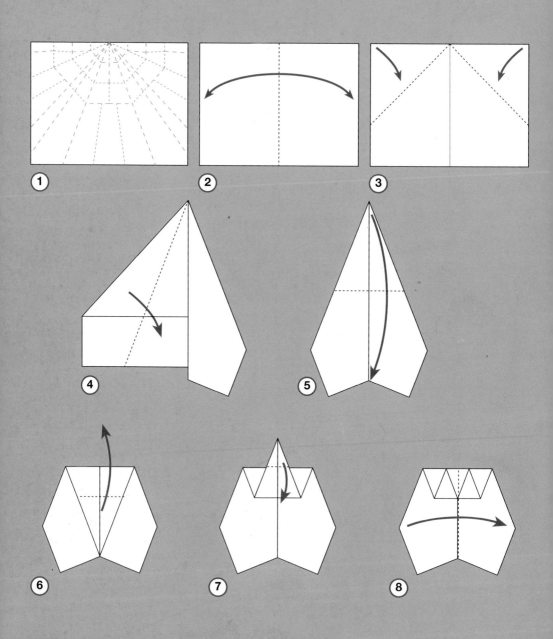

SINGLE SHEET FOLDED PLANES

Flight Path:	Flight Speed:	Throwing Technique:	Flight Correction:	trim view from rear
Swooping and aerobatic	Fast	Pinch the undersection at the front of the plane and throw normally. Throw vertically for loops	If plane drops, check wing level and flatten "cockpit" folds	

Wings need to be
very slightly raised

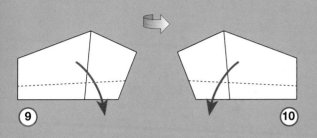

1. Start with paper turned landscape

2. Fold paper in half, then unfold to crease the center line

3. Fold down top corners to center crease

4. Fold down upper edges to center crease

5. Fold the top point down to the base of the center crease

6. Fold the point up

7. Fold the top point down to the base of the folded section

8. Fold the plane in half

9. Fold down the wing, turn the model over

10. Fold down the other wing. Flatten tail section and reshape wings to form the finished model

discus

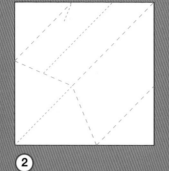

1

2

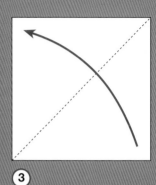

3

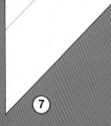

4

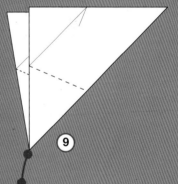

5

6

7

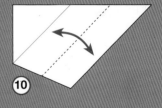

8

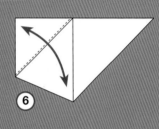

9

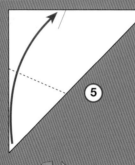

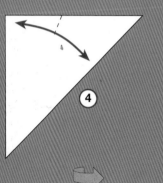

10

1. Cut the square template into four pieces. You will need two templates printed to make the eight segments

2. Start with one square

3. Fold paper in half along the diagonal

4. Pull the top corner to align with diagonal and make a short crease mark in the top edge

5. Fold up the bottom corner to the mark

30

Straight | Fast | Throw like a frisbee— hold the plane at the side with your arm curled round it. Flick your wrist outwards and release plane in one motion. For best flight, move your wrist down as well while doing the above action | The plane itself should not need correcting. The throwing technique can be tricky and may need practising for best flight |

Outer (and inner) edges bent slightly downwards

6. Fold down and unfold top left point of top layer to crease

7. Unfold bottom point and turn the model over

8. Repeat steps 4 to 7 for other side

9. Push bottom corner up between flaps. Make eight segments

10. Fold and unfold to crease

11. Insert point of one segment into another

12. When the segment is fully inserted, fold in the top points of the front segment to lock the segments together. Continue until all segments are inserted to make the complete disc

the flying fish

volans

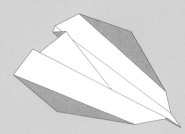

1. Start with paper turned portrait
2. Fold paper in half, then unfold to crease the center line
3. Fold down top corners almost to the center line
4. Fold down top point
5. Fold down top section
6. Fold down the top corners to the center crease and unfold
7. Fold down top corners to the crease mark just made and unfold

8. Fold top corners down and tuck under center flap
9. Turn the plane over
10. Fold the plane in half along the center crease
11. Fold down the wing (1) and fold up the wing tip (2)
12. Repeat for the other wing

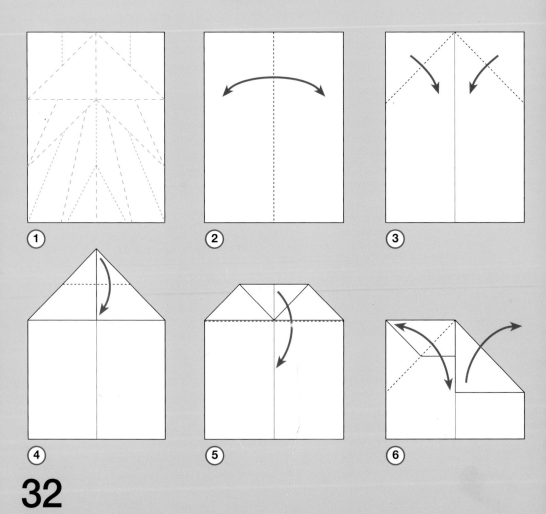

SINGLE SHEET FOLDED PLANES

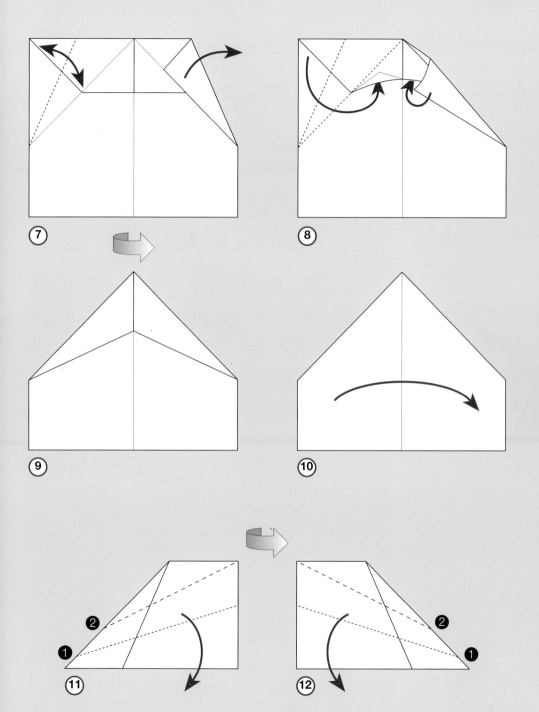

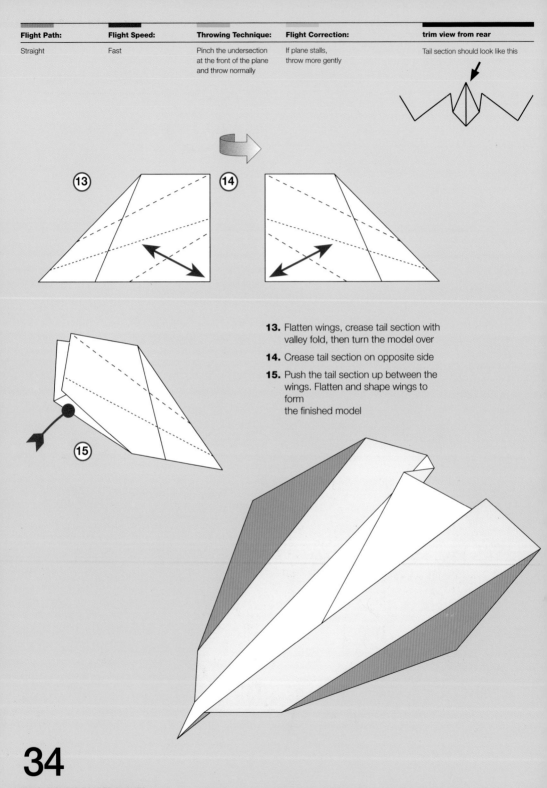

13. Flatten wings, crease tail section with valley fold, then turn the model over

14. Crease tail section on opposite side

15. Push the tail section up between the wings. Flatten and shape wings to form the finished model

15

1. Start with paper turned portrait

2. Fold paper in half, then unfold to crease the center line

3. Fold down top corners almost to the center line

4. Fold down top point

5. Turn the plane over

6. Fold down the top corners to the center line

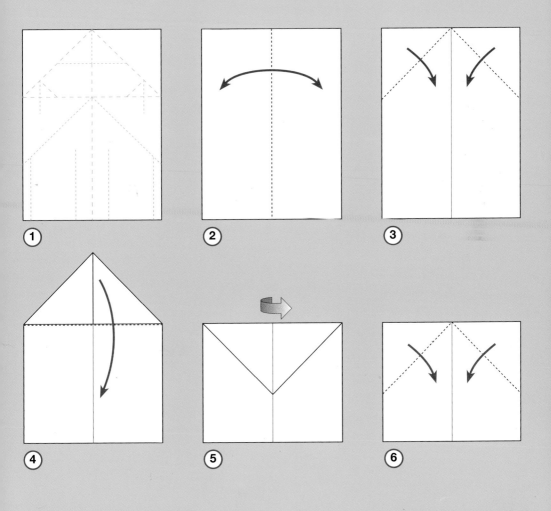

① ② ③

④ ⑤ ⑥

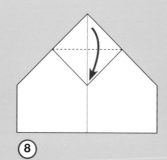

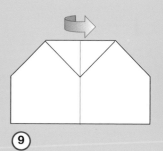

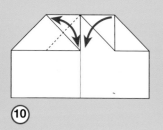

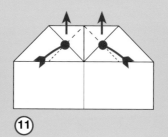

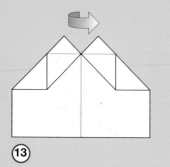

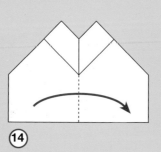

7. Turn the plane over

8. Fold down top point

9. Turn the plane over

10. Fold up corners from the center then down to crease

11. Push up midpoint of the diagonal flaps

12. Flatten new flaps

36

SINGLE SHEET FOLDED PLANES

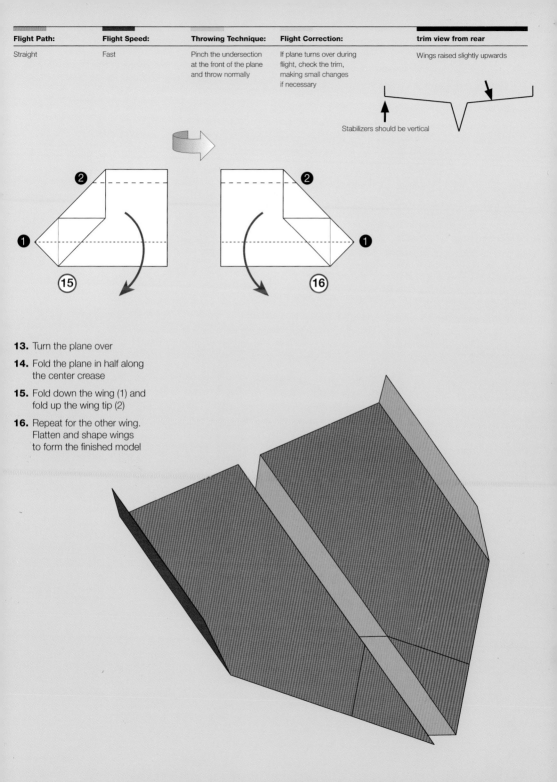

Flight Path:	Flight Speed:	Throwing Technique:	Flight Correction:	trim view from rear
Straight	Fast	Pinch the undersection at the front of the plane and throw normally	If plane turns over during flight, check the trim, making small changes if necessary	Wings raised slightly upwards

Stabilizers should be vertical

13. Turn the plane over

14. Fold the plane in half along the center crease

15. Fold down the wing (1) and fold up the wing tip (2)

16. Repeat for the other wing. Flatten and shape wings to form the finished model

the falcon

immusulus

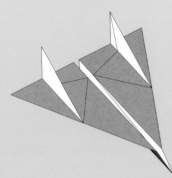

1. Start with paper turned portrait
2. Fold paper in half, then unfold to crease the center line
3. Fold the paper in half from the top
4. Fold down and unfold top corners to form creases from the center to bottom corners
5. Fold down and unfold top corners to meet diagonal creases

6. Push up midpoint of diagonal flaps
7. Flatten new flaps
8. Turn the plane over
9. Fold down top edges along the diagonal creases
10. Fold the plane in half along the center crease
11. Fold down the wing
12. Repeat for the other wing

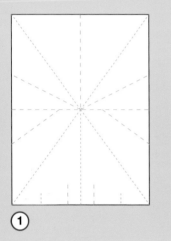

①

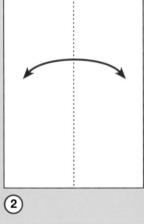

②

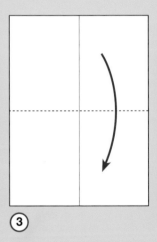

③

④

⑤

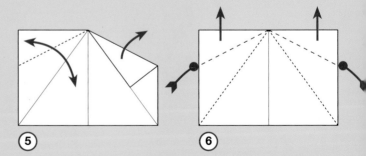

⑥

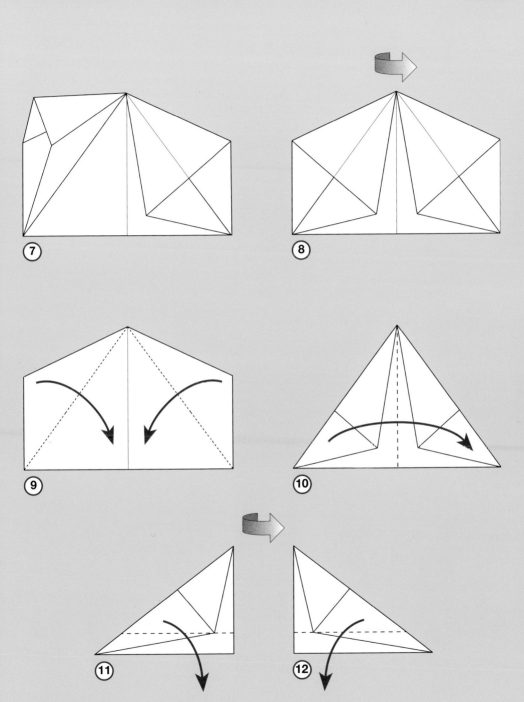

Flight Path:	Flight Speed:	Throwing Technique:	Flight Correction:	trim view from rear
Straight	Fast	Pinch the undersection at the front of the plane and throw normally	If the plane stalls or flips over, check the trim. The wings need to be raised as they level out during flight	Fins should point inwards

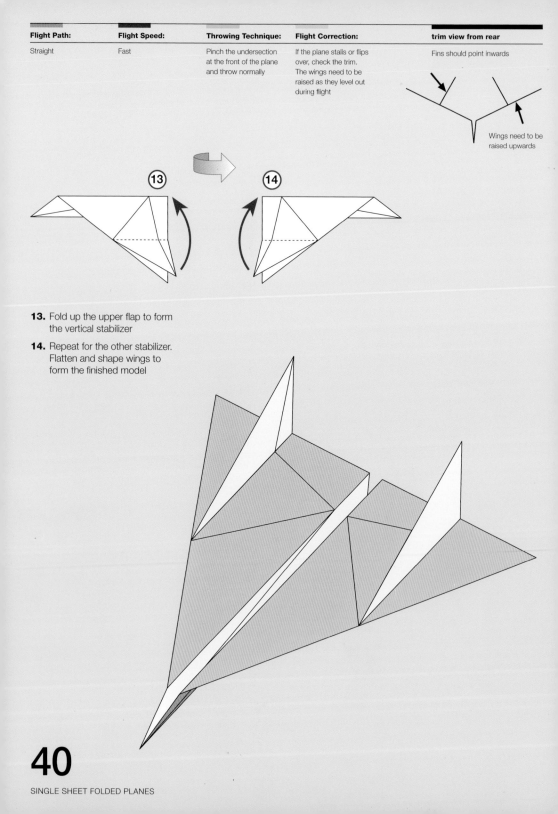

Wings need to be raised upwards

13. Fold up the upper flap to form the vertical stabilizer

14. Repeat for the other stabilizer. Flatten and shape wings to form the finished model

the ram
aries

1. Start with a square of paper
2. Fold paper in half, then unfold to crease the center line
3. Fold one side of the paper to the center crease and make a short marker crease
4. Fold down opposite top corners to marker crease
5. Fold down other top corner
6. Fold down top point

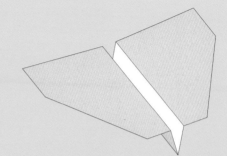

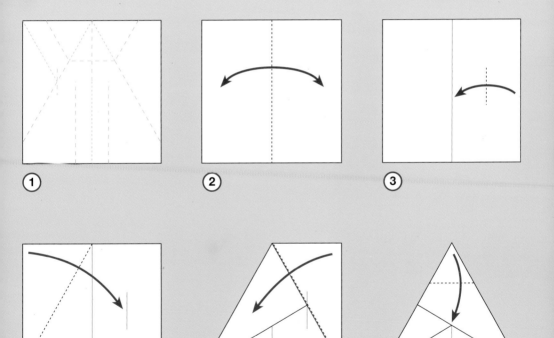

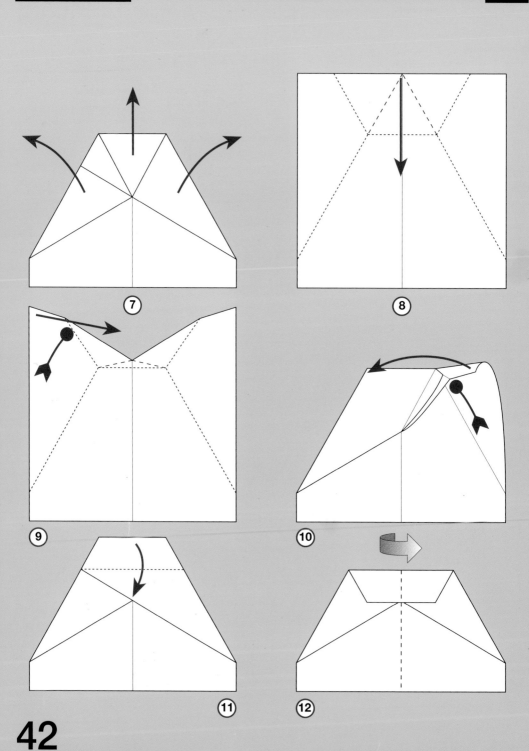

⑦ ⑧ ⑨ ⑩ ⑪ ⑫

42
SINGLE SHEET FOLDED PLANES

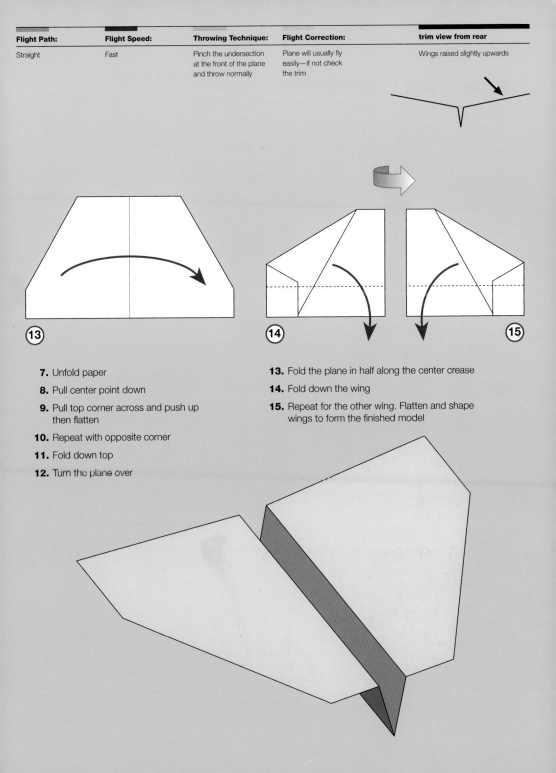

7. Unfold paper

8. Pull center point down

9. Pull top corner across and push up then flatten

10. Repeat with opposite corner

11. Fold down top

12. Turn the plane over

13. Fold the plane in half along the center crease

14. Fold down the wing

15. Repeat for the other wing. Flatten and shape wings to form the finished model

capricornus

1. Start with paper turned portrait
2. Fold paper in half, then unfold to crease the center line
3. Fold down top corners almost to the center line
4. Turn the plane over
5. Fold down the top point
6. Fold the top point back
7. Fold in top sections
8. Fold back part of section so that one point touches outer edge

9. Unfold stages 7 and 8 then fold the plane in half along the center crease
10. Fold down the main wing (1) and fold up the wing tip to crease (2)
11. Unfold the wings
12. Fold in wing edge sections (1) and (2) tucking them under the nose fold

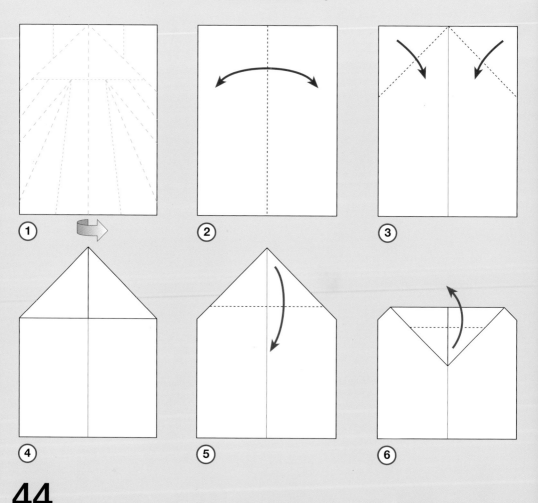

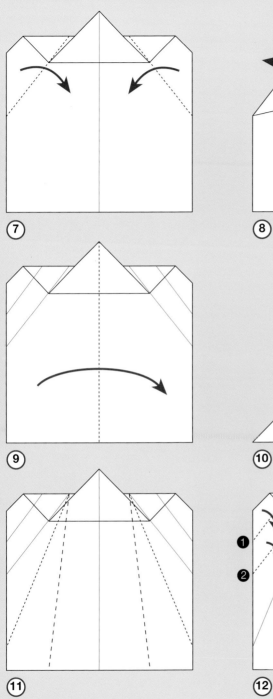
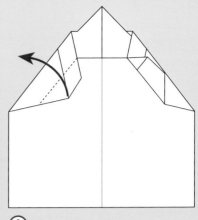
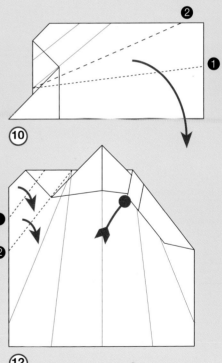

⑦ ⑧ ⑨ ⑩ ⑪ ⑫

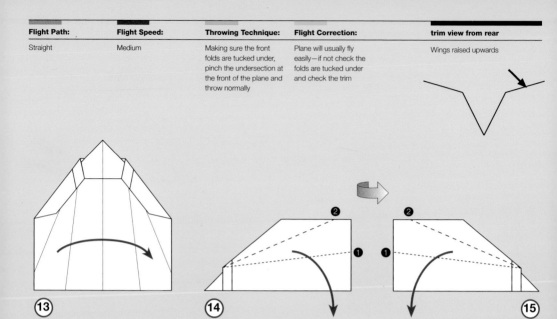

13. Fold the plane in half along the center crease

14. Fold down the main wing (1) and fold up the wing tip (2)

15. Repeat for the other wing. Flatten and shape wings to form the finished model

46

SINGLE SHEET FOLDED PLANES

the bat
vespertilio

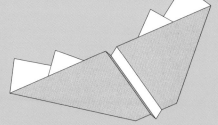

1. Start with paper turned landscape
2. Fold paper leaving a strip at the bottom
3. Fold paper in half, then unfold to crease the center line
4. Fold top corners to center line and unfold to crease
5. Fold down and unfold top corners to crease
6. Push corners to open up sides.

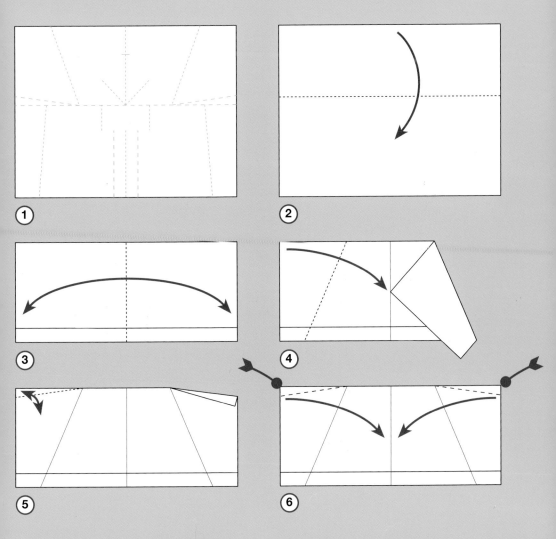

① ② ③ ④ ⑤ ⑥

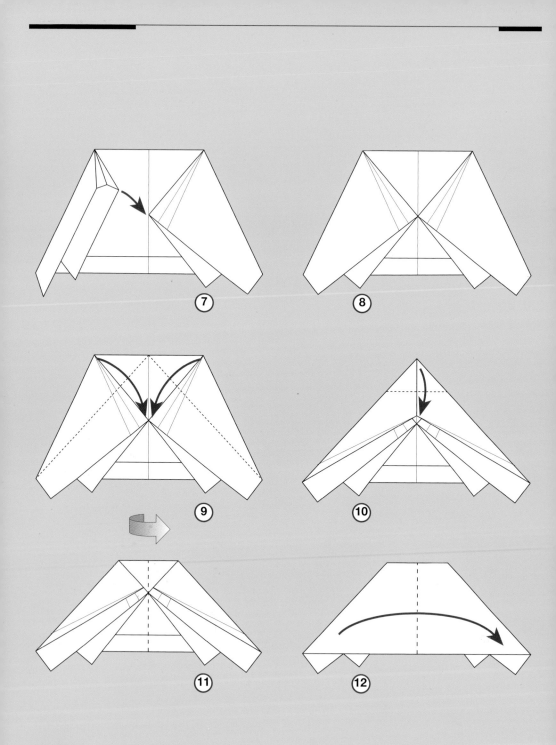

SINGLE SHEET FOLDED PLANES

Flight Path:	Flight Speed:	Throwing Technique:	Flight Correction:		trim view from rear
Straight	Medium	Pinch the undersection at the front of the plane and throw gently to normally	If plane dives, throw more gently. If plane swoops, check trim and throw more gently		Wings raised slightly upwards

⑬

⑭

7. Pull to center line

8. Flatten creases

9. Fold top corners to center line

10. Fold down the top point

11. Turn plane over

12. Fold the plane in half along the center crease

13. Fold down the wing, then turn the model over

14. Repeat for the other wing. Flatten tail section and reshape wings to form the finished model

dasyatis

1. Start with paper turned portrait
2. Fold and unfold top corner to crease
3. Fold and unfold opposite top corner to crease
4. Turn the plane over
5. Fold and unfold top edge
6. Push in sides and pull down top corners
7. Flatten folds

8. Fold top flap across to opposite side
9. Fold same corner up to top point
10. Fold top flap back across center
11. Fold other top flap across to opposite side
12. Fold same corner up to top point

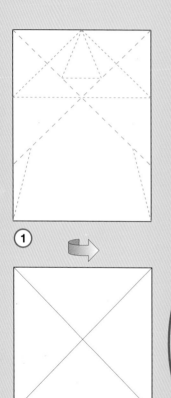
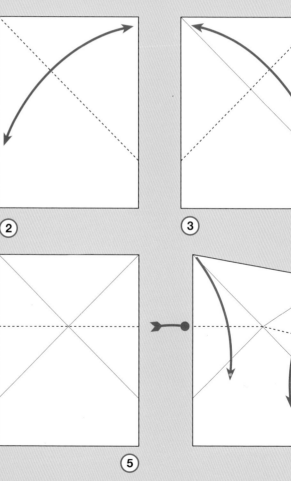

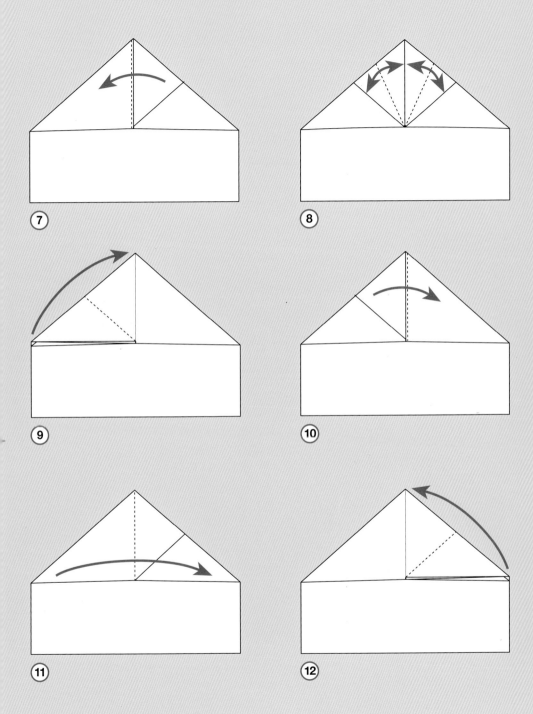

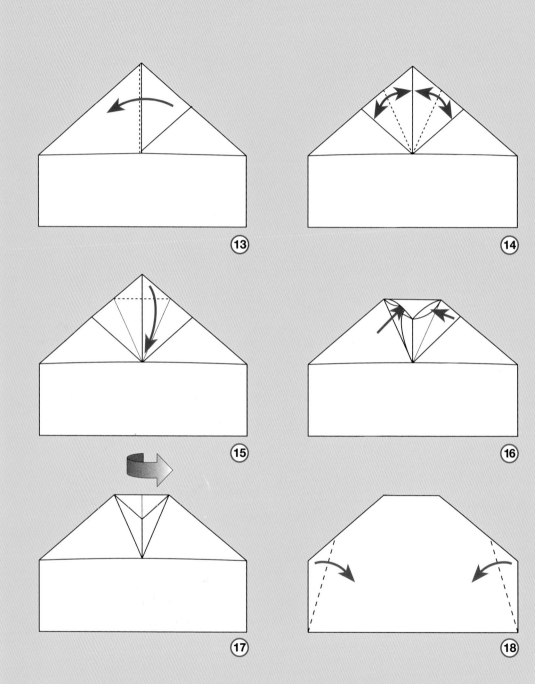

Flight Path:	Flight Speed:	Throwing Technique:	Flight Correction:	trim view from rear
Straight	Slow	Hold the folds underneath the front of the plane with your thumb and index/middle finger, and support the front edge of the plane with the tip of your ring finger. Throw gently OR Pinch the front edge between finger and thumb and flick your wrist as you let go of the plane. Throw gently	If plane dives, try altering the angle of the wing tips or bend the plane in half slightly	Wing tips raised upwards

Wing will curve downwards when holding

13. Fold top flap back across center

14. Fold top flaps to center line and unfold to crease

15. Fold down top point at crease marks

16. Tuck in side flaps to pockets of top flap

17. Turn the plane over

18. Fold up wing tips. Flatten and shape wings to form the finished model

the lion
leo

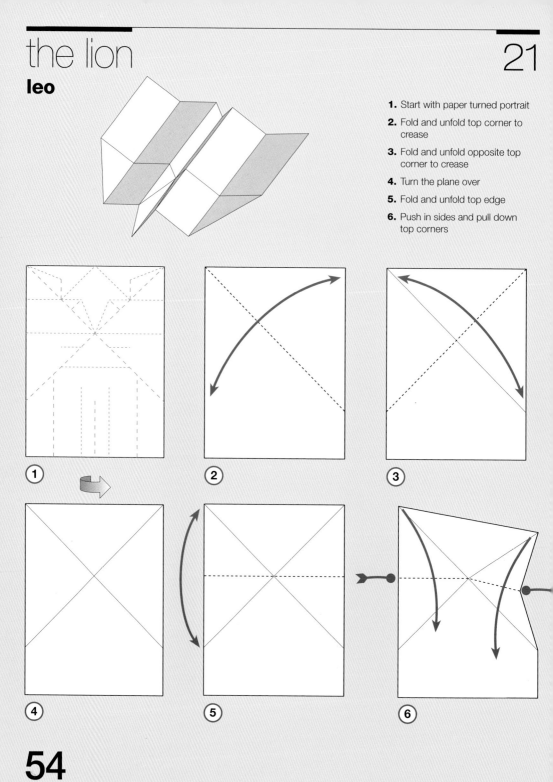

1. Start with paper turned portrait
2. Fold and unfold top corner to crease
3. Fold and unfold opposite top corner to crease
4. Turn the plane over
5. Fold and unfold top edge
6. Push in sides and pull down top corners

54
SINGLE SHEET FOLDED PLANES

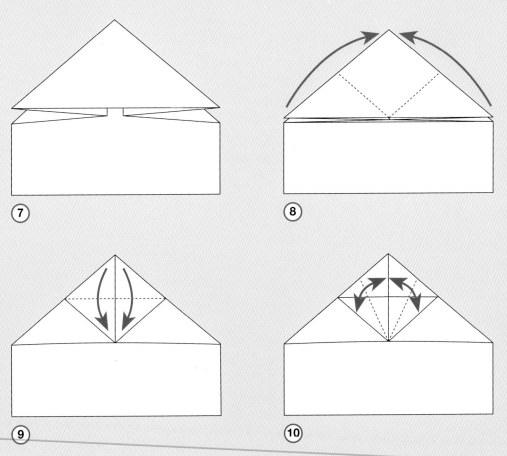

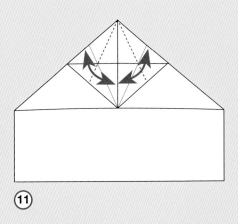

7. Flatten folds
8. Fold top flap outer corners to top point
9. Fold down two top points
10. Fold lower side flaps to center and unfold to crease
11. Fold upper side flaps to center and unfold to crease

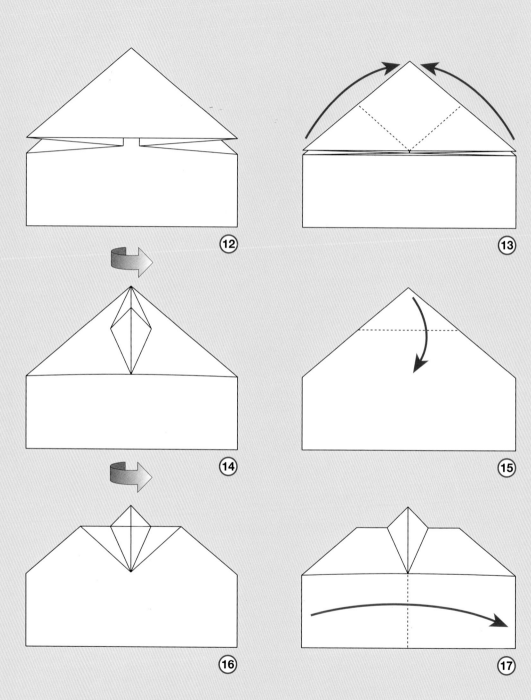

Flight Path:	Flight Speed:	Throwing Technique:	Flight Correction:	trim view from rear
Straight	Medium	Pinch the undersection at the front of the plane and throw normally	If plane is not flying well, make small adjustments to the trim and try again	Outer wing should be raised up steeply

Inner wing should be lowered downwards

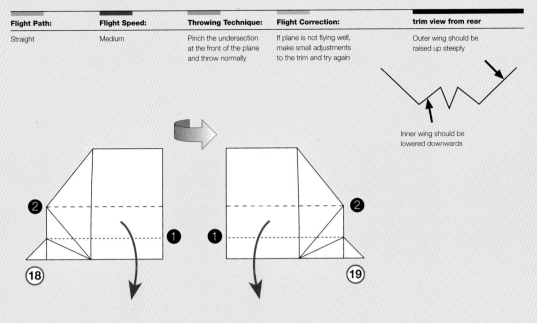

12. Push in upper edges of side flaps

13. Pull side points in to meet at center line

14. Turn the plane over

15. Fold down top point

16. Turn the plane over

17. Fold the plane in half

18. Fold down the wing (1) and fold up the outer wing (2)

19. Repeat for the other wing. Flatten and shape wings to form the finished model

sagitta

1. Cut the paper as shown
2. Fold and unfold square piece to opposite corner
3. Fold and unfold opposite top corner to crease
4. Turn the plane over
5. Fold and unfold top edge
6. Push in sides and pull down top corners
7. Flatten folds
8. Fold top flap outer corners to top point

9. Fold lower side flaps to center and unfold to crease
10. Fold top points out
11. Fold top flaps down
12. Fold down outer point of one flap and fold that flap across to opposite edge
13. Fold other flap over
14. Fold and tuck in top point of front flap
15. Flatten folds

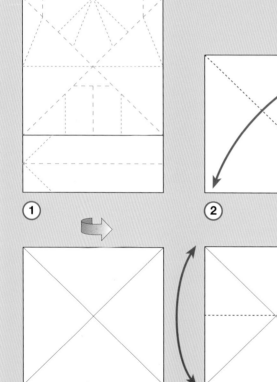

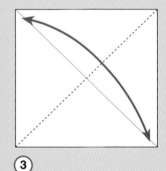

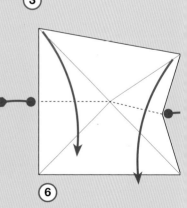

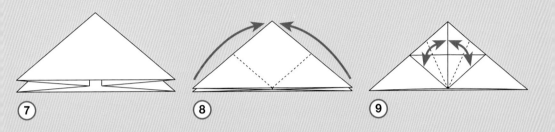

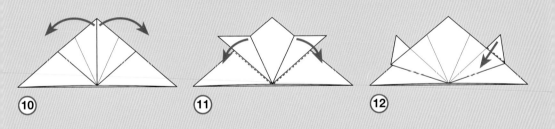

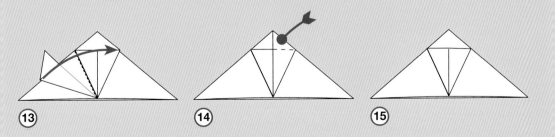

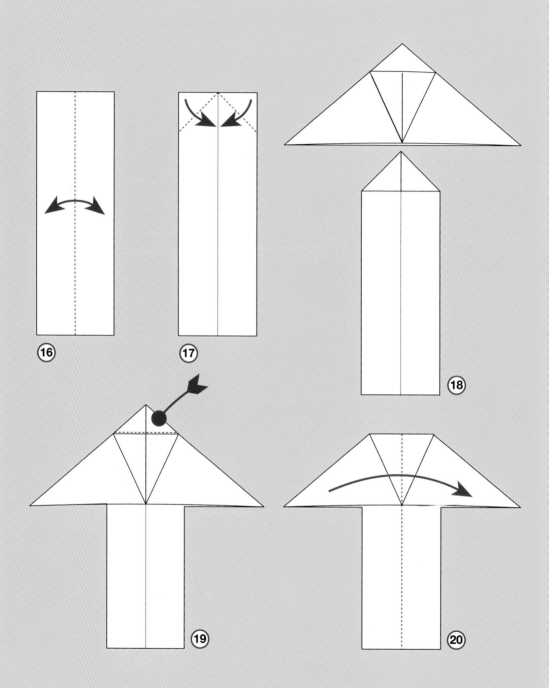

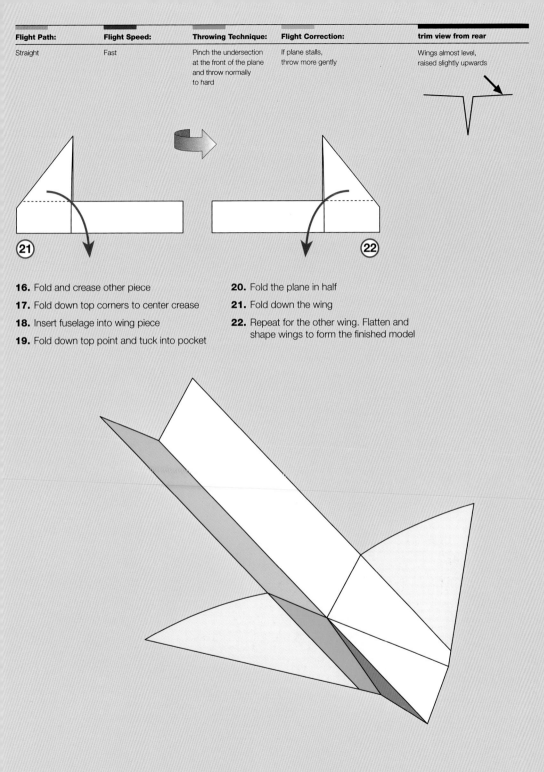

16. Fold and crease other piece

17. Fold down top corners to center crease

18. Insert fuselage into wing piece

19. Fold down top point and tuck into pocket

20. Fold the plane in half

21. Fold down the wing

22. Repeat for the other wing. Flatten and shape wings to form the finished model

the spike
clavus

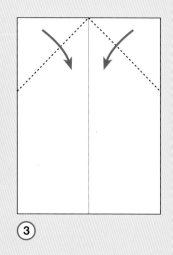

1. Start with paper turned portrait
2. Fold paper in half, then unfold to crease the center line
3. Fold down top corners almost to the center line
4. Fold down the top point
5. Fold down top corners to the center line and unfold to crease
6. Pull mid point of top flap to opposite crease

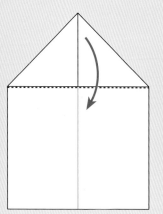

①

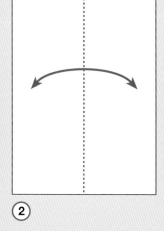

②

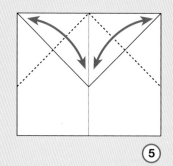

③

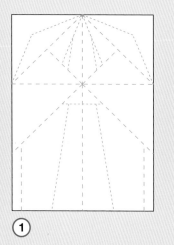

④

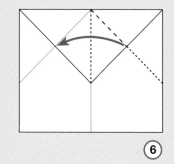

⑤

⑥

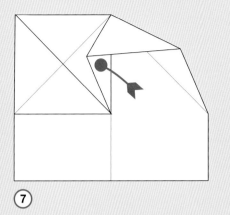

(7)

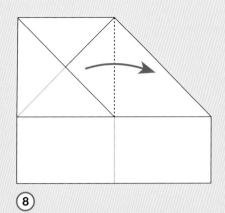

(8)

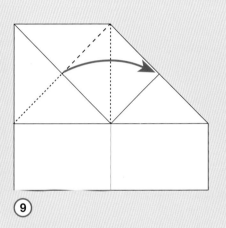

(9)

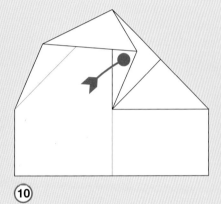

(10)

7. Push to open then flatten

8. Pull top flap back

9. Pull mid point of top flap to opposite crease

10. Push to open then flatten

11. Pull top flap back

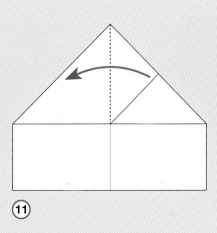

(11)

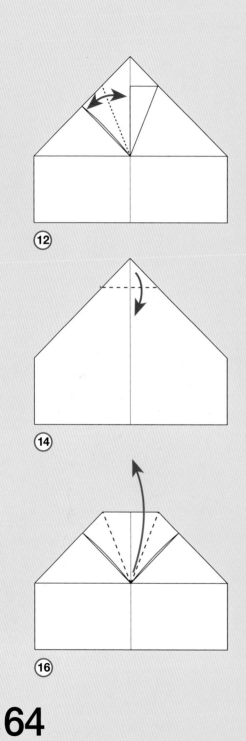

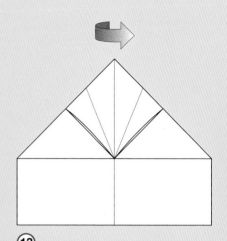

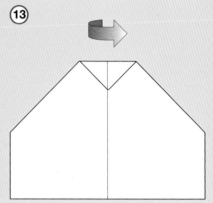

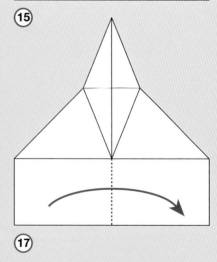

64
SINGLE SHEET FOLDED PLANES

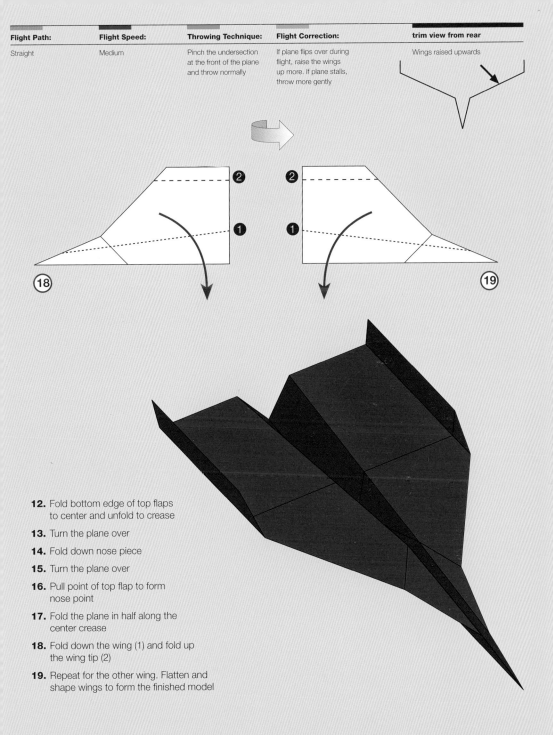

12. Fold bottom edge of top flaps to center and unfold to crease

13. Turn the plane over

14. Fold down nose piece

15. Turn the plane over

16. Pull point of top flap to form nose point

17. Fold the plane in half along the center crease

18. Fold down the wing (1) and fold up the wing tip (2)

19. Repeat for the other wing. Flatten and shape wings to form the finished model

the fire

ardor

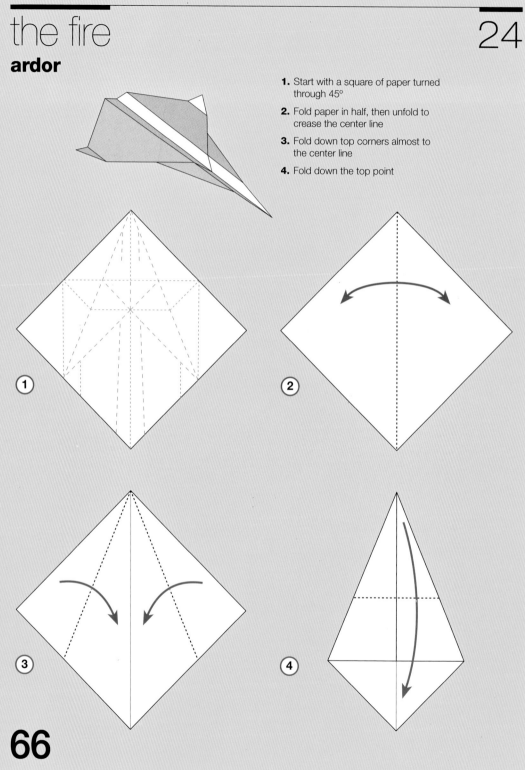

1. Start with a square of paper turned through 45°
2. Fold paper in half, then unfold to crease the center line
3. Fold down top corners almost to the center line
4. Fold down the top point

5. Fold down two top corners and unfold to crease

6. Start to pull top corner across

7. Push to open up flap while pulling corner across

8. Flatten the fold then fold the top flap back across the center crease

9. 10. 11. Repeat for opposite corner

12. Fold up flap

13. Flatten all creases then unfold completely

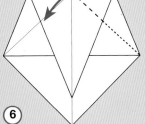

(5)

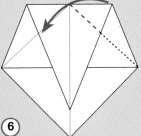

(6)

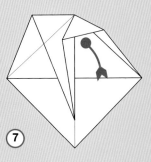

(7)

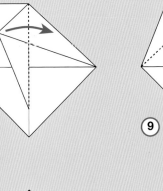

(8)

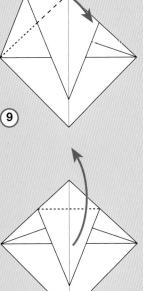

(9)

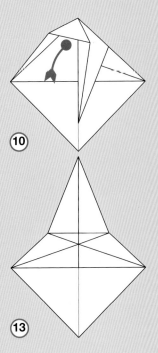

(10)

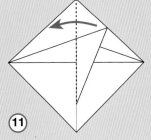

(11)

(12)

(13)

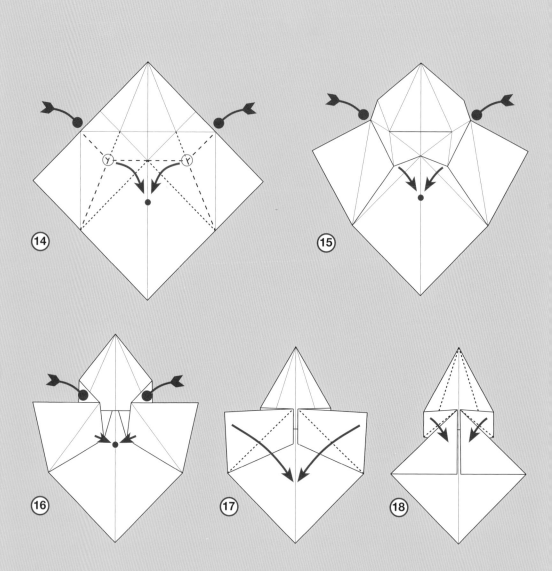

The tricky part

14. 15. 16. Holding upper edges and pushing from behind, bring circled points down to marked point. This will pull nose piece in and down

17. Fold side flaps in

18. Fold down side flaps of nose piece

19. Turn the model over

20. Fold down wing (1) and fold up wing flap (2)

21. Repeat for other wing. Reshape wings and trim to form the finished model

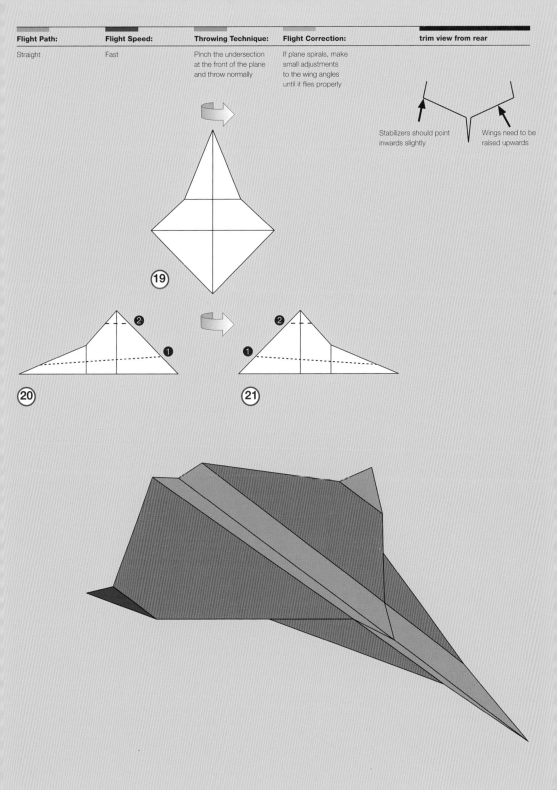

Stabilizers should point inwards slightly

Wings need to be raised upwards

delphinus

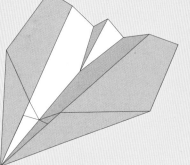

1. Start with paper turned portrait

2. Fold paper in half, then unfold to crease the center line

3. Fold down top corners almost to the center line

4. Fold down the top point

5. Fold top right point to center crease

6. Pull top left point to center crease and flatten

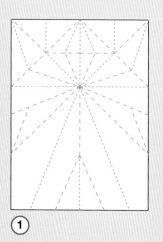

①

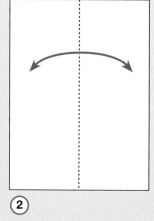

②

③

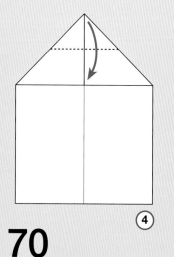

④

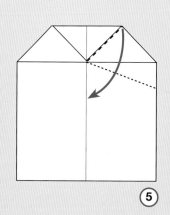

⑤

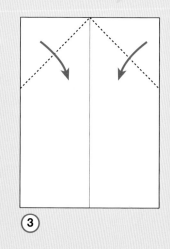

⑥

70

SINGLE SHEET FOLDED PLANES

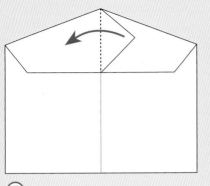

(7)

(8)

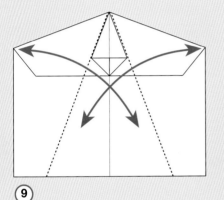

(9)

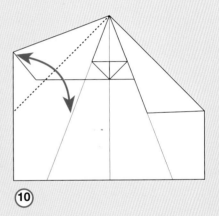

(10)

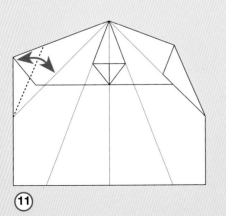

(11)

7. Fold flap across center line to crease

8. With flap vertical push down to flatten either side of center

9. Fold and unfold wings to crease

10. Fold down corner to align with crease and unfold

11. Fold down corner to align with new crease and unfold

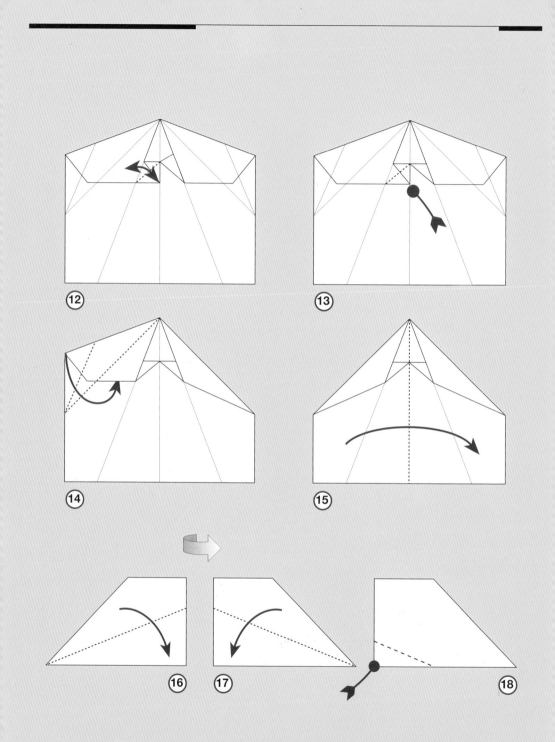

SINGLE SHEET FOLDED PLANES

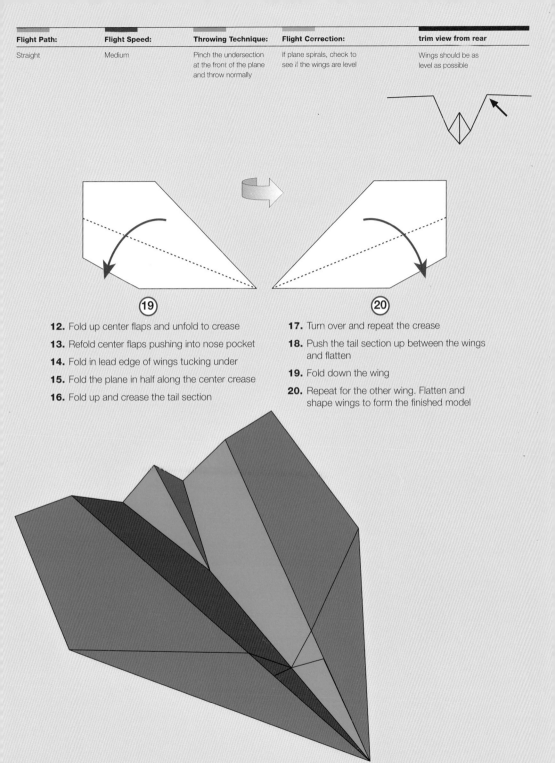

(19)

12. Fold up center flaps and unfold to crease

13. Refold center flaps pushing into nose pocket

14. Fold in lead edge of wings tucking under

15. Fold the plane in half along the center crease

16. Fold up and crease the tail section

(20)

17. Turn over and repeat the crease

18. Push the tail section up between the wings and flatten

19. Fold down the wing

20. Repeat for the other wing. Flatten and shape wings to form the finished model

part 2
single sheet
cut-out planes

74

hexagonum

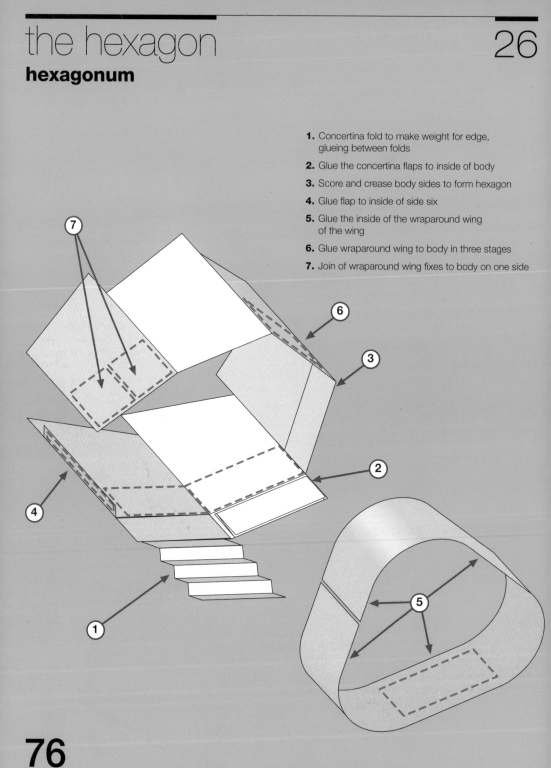

1. Concertina fold to make weight for edge, glueing between folds
2. Glue the concertina flaps to inside of body
3. Score and crease body sides to form hexagon
4. Glue flap to inside of side six
5. Glue the inside of the wraparound wing of the wing
6. Glue wraparound wing to body in three stages
7. Join of wraparound wing fixes to body on one side

Flight Path:	Flight Speed:	Throwing Technique:	Flight Correction:	trim view from rear
Straight then sudden change of direction	Fast	Hold the plane lightly between thumb and middle finger then throw forward sharply while twisting the wrist to give spin	Check symmetry— throwing technique may need practice	Should be symmetrical

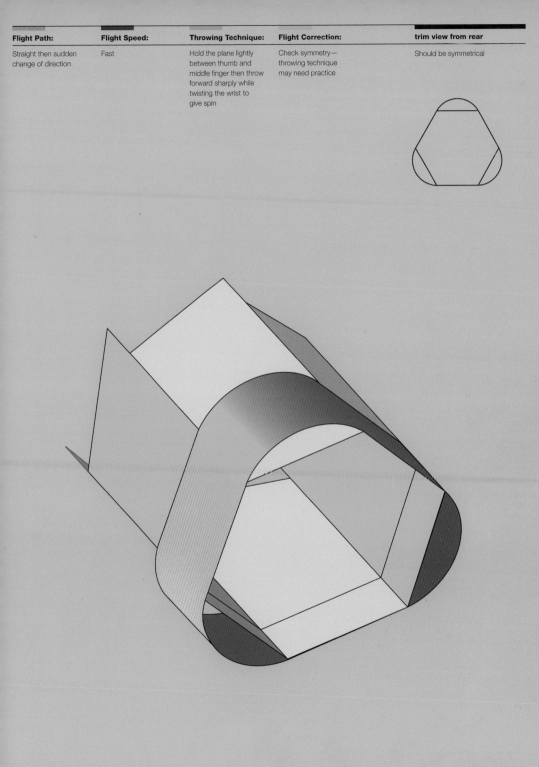

scorpius

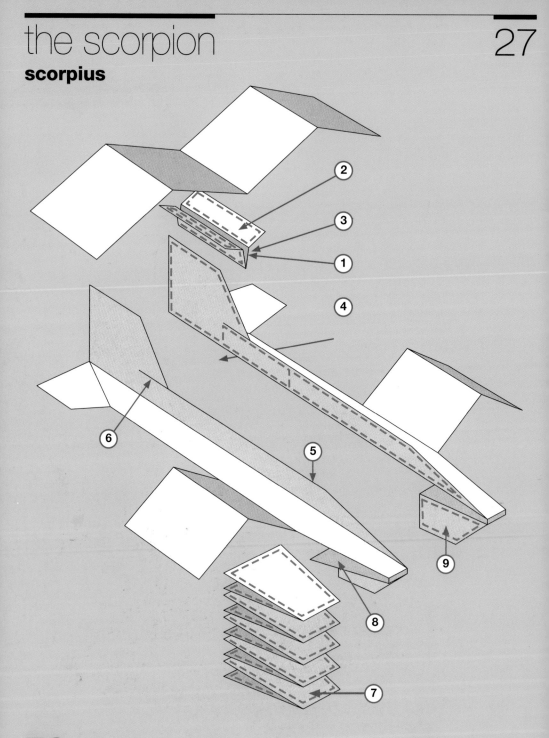

Flight Path:	Flight Speed:	Throwing Technique:	Flight Correction:	trim view from rear
Straight	Fast	Hold the plane by the launching tab and throw gently but firmly	Check symmetry	Wings should be angled

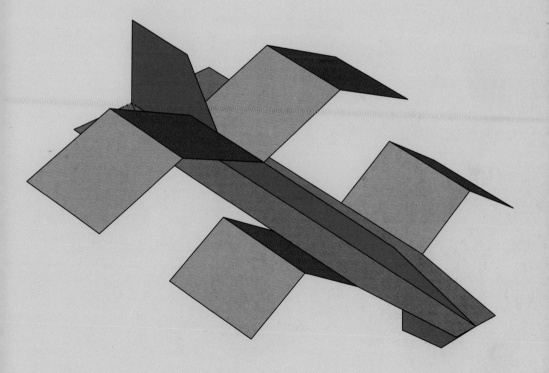

1. Glue together the bottom part of the wing holder

2. Glue the wing holder to the underside of the back wing

3. Glue this side of the wing holder (bottom part only, not top flap)

4. Push the rear wing through the slot on this piece sticking the wing holder to the inside of the fuselage

5. Glue the inside edge of this piece

6. Push the wing through the slot and then stick the two halves of the plane together

7. Glue together the nose weight parts as shown

8. Glue the nose weights in the space between the front flaps and the bottom of the plane

9. Glue together the holding piece

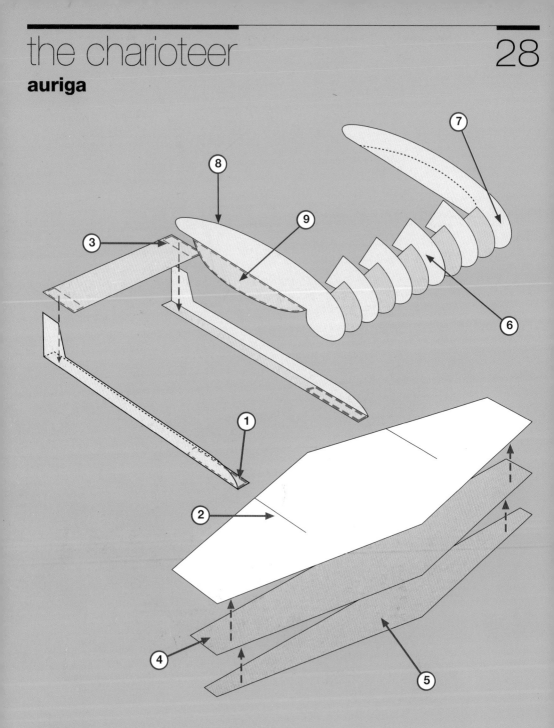

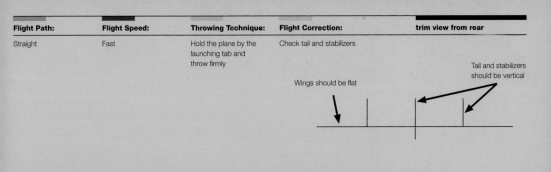

Wings should be flat

Tail and stabilizers should be vertical

1. Glue the side parts where shown

2. Insert each side part into the slots in the wing, sticking the glued parts underneath

3. Glue the ends of the tail and stick them onto the back of the side pieces

4. Glue the wider wing stabilizer underneath the front of the wing

5. Glue the thinner wing stabilizer over the previous one, underneath the front of the wing

6. Glue together the nose weight, alternating the large and small parts

7. Stick the weight to the inside of one of the body pieces

8. Glue along the inside of the other body piece and stick the body together

9. Glue the flaps on the body pieces and stick the body to the top of the wing

pilum

1. Glue together the body, keeping the edge with the marks on the outside

2. Fold up the nose weight adding spots of glue at the end to hold it together.

3. Glue the nose weight into the front end of the body

4. Glue all of the inside edge of the tail section

5. Wrap the tail around the back end of the body as shown and press it together

Flight Path:	Flight Speed:	Throwing Technique:	Flight Correction:	trim view from rear
Straight	Fast	Hold the plane by the launching tab and throw gently but firmly	Adjust curve and/or bend wings up slightly	Wings should be gently curved

Tail plane should bend down slightly

6. Add some glue to the underside of the body in between the marks

7. Stick the wing section to the body, lining it up with the marks

8. Fold up the wings and curve them slightly as shown in the diagram

libra

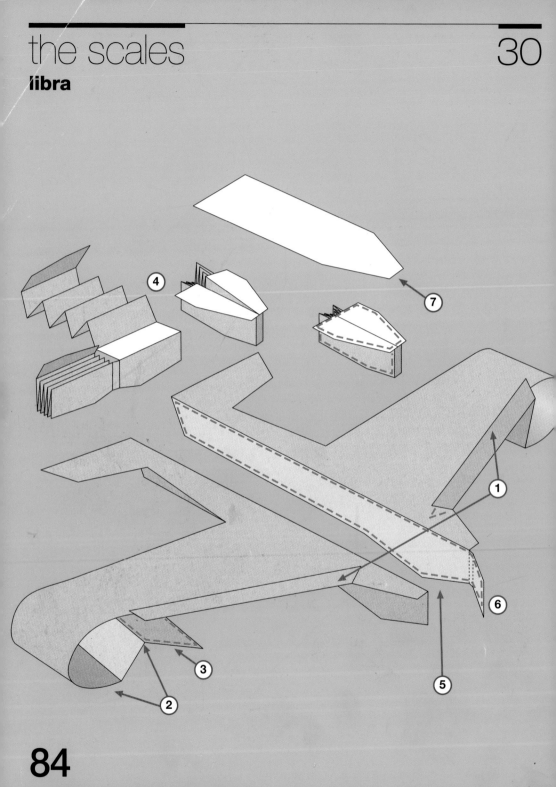

SINGLE SHEET CUT-OUT PLANES

Flight Path:	Flight Speed:	Throwing Technique:	Flight Correction:	trim view from rear
Straight	Medium	Hold the plane by the launching tab and throw gently but firmly	Check symmetry and trim	Wings should be angled up slightly

Wing ends should be
smoothly curved and symmetrical

1. Fold over and glue down the wing reinforcing strips

2. Fold the wing tip segments to a right-angle

3. Glue the wing end to the underside of the main wing, making a smooth curve of the wing end

4. Concertina fold the nose weight, trapping the two sets of folds

5. Slot nose weight between the fuselage parts and glue the fuselage together

6. Wrap nose flap around front of nose weight and glue to outside of opposite fuselage

7. Glue the reinforcing strip to the top of the plane

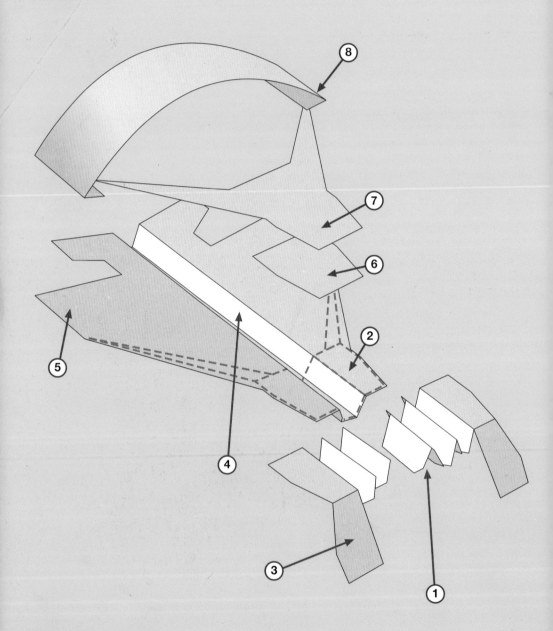

Flight Path:	Flight Speed:	Throwing Technique:	Flight Correction:	trim view from rear
Straight	Fast	Hold the undersection at the front of the plane and throw normally	If plane stalls, bend the ends of the tail down slightly	

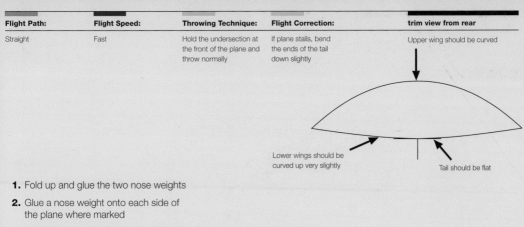

Upper wing should be curved

Lower wings should be curved up very slightly

Tail should be flat

1. Fold up and glue the two nose weights

2. Glue a nose weight onto each side of the plane where marked

3. Glue the front flaps of the nose weights under the front of the plane

4. Glue along the inside of the plane and stick the middle together

5. Stick the arch onto the plane, lining the flaps up with the edges of the wings

6. Stick the small reinforcing section to the underside of the larger reinforcing section

7. Stick the large reinforcing section onto the front of the plane

8. Glue the flaps on the arch

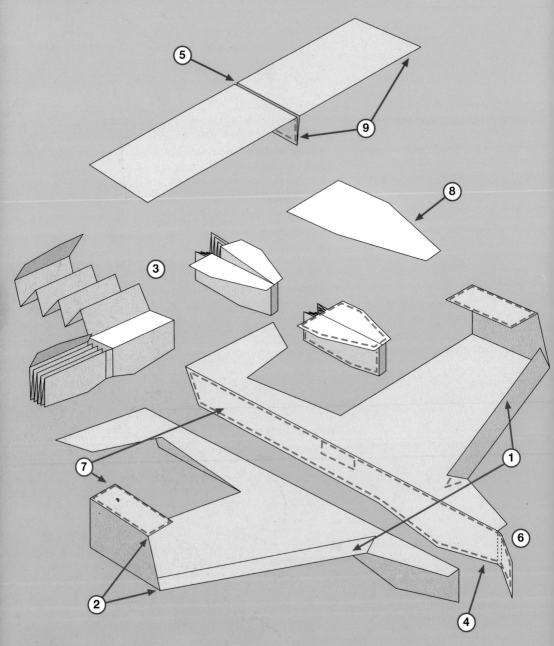

Flight Path:	Flight Speed:	Throwing Technique:	Flight Correction:	trim view from rear
Straight	Medium	Hold the undersection at the front of the plane and throw normally	Make sure trim is symmetrical	Upper wings should be curved

Lower wings and tail need to be level

1. Fold over and glue down the wing reinforcing strips

2. Fold the wing tip support segments to right-angles

3. Concertina fold the nose weight, trapping the two sets of folds

4. Glue nose weight to one side of fuselage

5. Fold center of upper wing and glue together

6. Wrap nose flap around front of nose weight and glue to outside of opposite fuselage

7. Glue fuselage together and the upper wing to the wing tip support segment

8. Glue the reinforcing strip to the top of the nose of the plane

9. Glue vertical segment of upper wing to one side of fuselage and to corresponding wing tip support

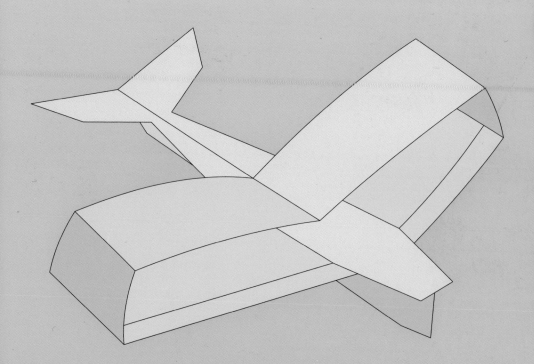

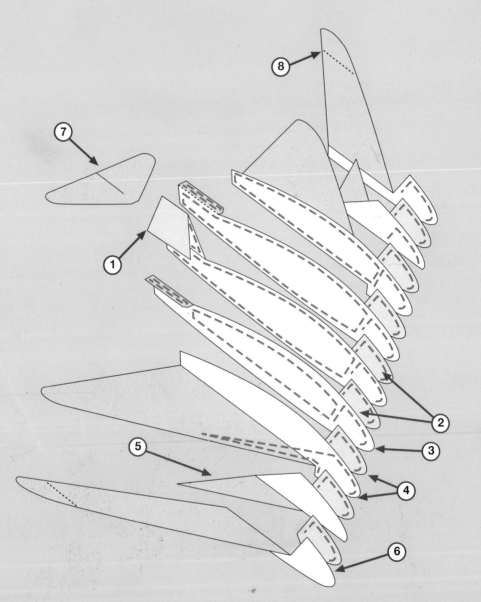

1. Fold down and glue tail section
2. Glue a weight onto each side of the fuselage
3. Glue the side sections onto each side of the fuselage
4. Glue a weight onto each side of the main wing sections then glue to fuselage
5. Glue upper wing supports onto the plane on top of main wing
6. Glue a weight onto each of the large wing supports, then fix supports onto the underside of the wing
7. Slot the tail piece into the slit on the plane and stick the flaps underneath to the bottom of it to hold it in place
8. Fold up wing tips

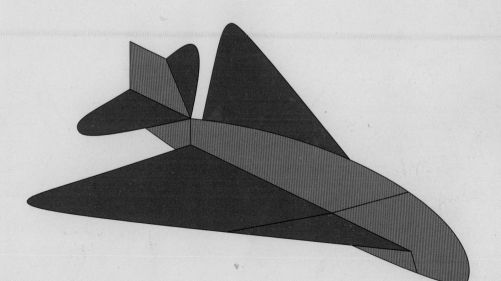

triangulum

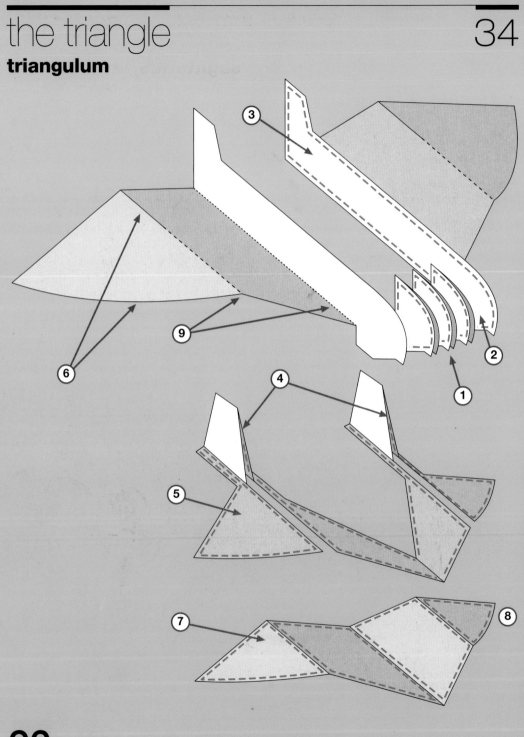

SINGLE SHEET CUT-OUT PLANES

Flight Path:	Flight Speed:	Throwing Technique:	Flight Correction:	trim view from rear
Straight	Medium	Hold the undersection at the front of the plane and throw normally	If plane turns over during flight, bend the outer wings up a little—adjust a little at a time	Outer wing bends down

Inner part of wing bends up

1. Fold and glue each nose weight then stick them together to form one weight

2. Stick the weight onto one side of the fuselage

3. Glue along the fuselage and stick the two halves together

4. Glue the side fins together

5. Glue along the top of the fin section

6. Push the fins through the slots in the wings and stick the fin section underneath, lining it up with the front of the wings

7. Glue across the top of the wing support

8. Stick the wing support to the underside of the fin segment, lining it up with the front of the wing

9. Bend the wings up at the fuselage and mountain fold in line with the fins

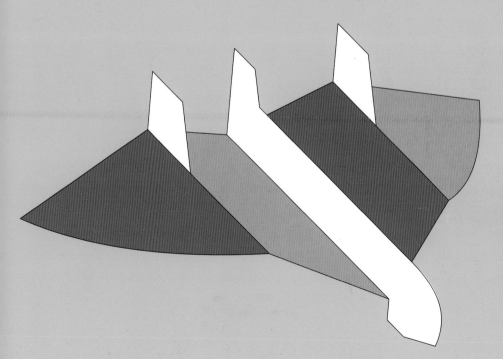

phoenix

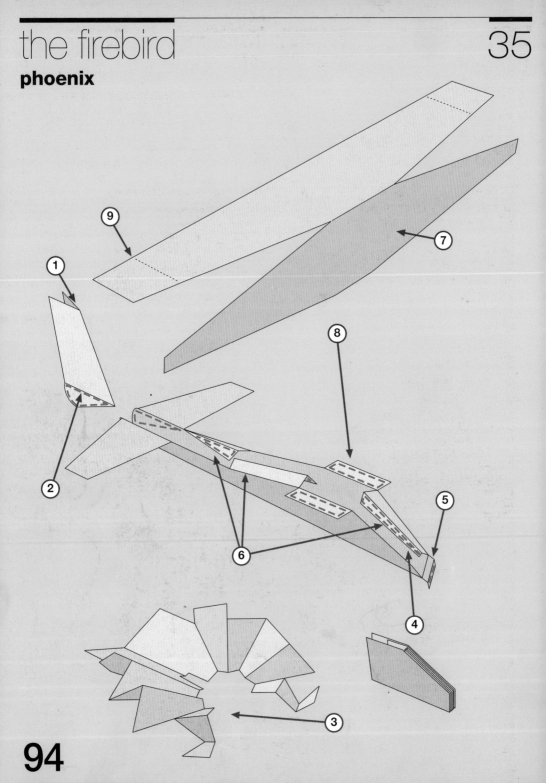

SINGLE SHEET CUT-OUT PLANES

Flight Path:	Flight Speed:	Throwing Technique:	Flight Correction:	trim view from rear
Straight	Medium	Hold the undersection at the front of the plane and throw normally	If plane dives, throw more gently	Wing tips need to be raised slightly upwards

1. Glue the tail section together

2. Glue the bottom of tail section on both sides where marked and stick it to the inside of the fuselage

3. Fold up the nose weight, gluing all the sections together

4. Glue the nose weight on the inside of the body

5. Glue the nose tab and fix it to the weight

6. Glue the three tabs along the fuselage, fold over and fix to opposite side

7. Fold the wing support back and glue it to the underside of the wing

8. Stick the wing onto the wing tabs

9. Fold up wing tips

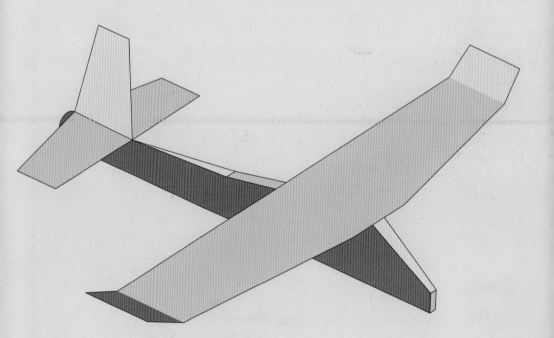

afterword

I make no claim to have originated all these planes and other flying devices. There are very many planes and plane makers and, besides producing my own, I have been inspired by others' designs, as I hope you may be inspired to adapt and develop the models in this publication.

For further reading, I recommend *The Great International Paper Airplane Book* by Jerry Mander, George Dippel and Howard Gossage, a book about the background to, and results of, a competition run by *Scientific American* in 1966 to find the world's best paper airplanes. The competition drew entries from around the globe and generated some fascinating and innovative designs.

acknowledgments

Thanks to Denise Goodey for loyal intervention. Special thanks to Amy Trotman for invaluable assistance. Without her intelligence and diligent commitment in making up, testing, and drawing so many models, and their variations, this project might never have flown. Also thanks to Felix Bounford for his creativity and lateral thinking.

96